Frank James Mathew

Defender of the Faith

A Romance

Frank James Mathew

Defender of the Faith
A Romance

ISBN/EAN: 9783337007409

Printed in Europe, USA, Canada, Australia, Japan

Cover: Foto ©Thomas Meinert / pixelio.de

More available books at **www.hansebooks.com**

DEFENDER OF THE FAITH ❧ *A Romance*

BY

FRANK MATHEW

WITH THREE PORTRAITS AFTER HOLBEIN

JOHN LANE: THE BODLEY HEAD
LONDON AND NEW YORK
1899

Portraits

Note .

THIS book deals with the history of Henry the Eighth as seen by Henry Percy, sixth Earl of Northumberland, who was Wolsey's pupil, Anne Bullen's lover, and the King's friend. All the chief characters—except Lady Northumberland—are drawn from historical models. Many of the words ascribed to them are taken from historical documents; for instance, Wolsey's words are mainly derived from Cavendish's "Life of Wolsey," and Anne Bullen's words in the Tower are based on

Note

Kingston's "Memorial." The writer adopts Chapuys' explanation of Anne Bullen's fall. Few of the scenes are historical. Aske was not present when Northumberland arrested the Cardinal. Northumberland died during the Rising of the Pilgrims of Grace. The King was not at the Council on the day of Cromwell's arrest. The writer differs from Froude's opinion that Cromwell was honest in his profession of piety. Other students believe he had no religion. It is known that he had been fervent in his profession of Roman Catholicism when that was convenient. The writer has used the "State Papers," the "Baga de Secretis," Strype, Godwin, Constantyne, the "Cabala," and other authorities.

Contents

Defender of the Faith

BOOK I

The Fall of the Cross

CHAPTER I

DRUMS muttering in the twilight startled the citizens of York. Northumberland riding slowly at the head of his gentlemen was aware of dim faces at the shadowy windows. As he reached the Cathedral he saw thousands of horsemen ranked about banners. All were turned to him, and so was a man waiting at the foot of the steps.

"It is dusk," said Northumberland as he stopped by the door.

1

Defender of the Faith

"Is it nightfall or dawn?" the man said without stirring.

"God knows," said Northumberland.

"My lords," said the other, lifting his voice, "the Earl of Northumberland, our captain, is here."

"Robert Aske," said Northumberland, "your voice is familiar."

As he held out his hand Aske gripped it, and answered, "I was told you might come."

"Where do we go?"

"To Cawood."

"Why do we set out with an army?"

"To overawe the people," said Aske.

Northumberland turned his horse's head as a charger was brought up and Aske mounted. Then he rode down the street with Aske on his left. The long muster clattered behind them as

2

The Fall of the Cross

they passed through the ramparts and took the road to the South.

"We go to arrest Cardinal Wolsey?" Northumberland said when they had ridden some way.

"You are to arrest him of treason when I lift my right hand."

"When the King's messenger brought me secret orders to head the force I would find waiting in York and to accompany the man who would answer me as you did, I had a foreboding of mischief. This is Cromwell's work?"

"Mistress Anne's, rather. She hates Wolsey because he knelt to the King and implored him to beware of her wiles."

"What news from London?"

"The Pope still refuses to declare the marriage with Queen Catherine void. It is said the King is about to call himself the Head of the Church of England."

Defender of the Faith

"And marry Mistress Anne?" said Northumberland.

"It is probable."

"Does she seem happy?"

"She spends most of her time laughing and dancing. 'With these dances of hers,' said More to me lately, 'she will spurn off our heads like footballs. Before long her own head will dance the same dance as ours.'"

"She has risen to a dangerous eminence while I kept aloof. Now I am married. You know my wife?"

"The Lady Magdalen and I were playmates in our childhood," said Aske.

"Because my marriage offended some one mighty at Court I am given this unwelcome command. Cromwell feared I would hesitate, so he sent those dark orders. Yet Wolsey is fallen. I fancied they would leave him unharmed."

The Fall of the Cross

"Since his disgrace he has won the love of the people. The clergy meant to install him in the Cathedral next Sunday. While he lives he is dangerous. Should Mistress Anne sulk or ill news come from abroad, the King bellows, 'Norris, take this ring to the Cardinal, and tell him I love him!'"

"Have you seen Norris lately?"

"No. He is seldom away from Mistress Anne's side."

"I am sorry to hear it. He is so reckless and boastful."

"He talks wildly; but the King is his friend."

"It is unsafe to cross the King when he loves," said Northumberland. "So the Cardinal learnt. How can they convict him of treason?"

"With the help of Doctor Augustine."

"The Italian wizard?"

Defender of the Faith

"Now physician at Court. The King told him to mend the Cardinal's health. 'Whatever disease he may have,' said Augustine, 'if your Majesty desires his death, you may be secure; I can promise he will not live for three days.' But the King flew in a rage and thumped the table and shouted, 'I had rather lose twenty thousand pounds. You must cure him.'"

"Augustine is a poisoner, then?"

"So it is said. His Majesty has a horror of poison. Else we would all go in terror of that subtle Venetian."

"Then he is at Cawood now?" said the Earl.

"So I think."

"Are we to keep the Cardinal there?"

"I have a task to perform. Then you are to arrest him, and I am to hand him over to Kingston."

"The Constable of the Tower!"

The Fall of the Cross

" You and I are forbidden to speak with Wolsey apart."

" I thought they distrusted me," said Northumberland.

" They doubt me too."

" Then why were you sent? "

" Because my errand is legal and I am noted as an adherent to Rome."

" Cromwell does credit to his favourite teacher, Machiavelli. How the knave prospers! When I knew him first he was a money-lender. To repay his assistance I introduced him to Wolsey. The Cardinal was then in his glory. You were at the banquet he gave on Hallowe'en at Westminster? It was three years ago."

" I was not there."

" I forgot. Remote among books in the Temple, you avoided our gaieties. Because to-night is Hallowe'en I was

Defender of the Faith

thinking of it as I rode into York. It was worth seeing. The Red Room was ablaze with candles while hundreds of his gentlemen feasted in crimson velvet with shining ladies and the ranks of his yeomen surrounded us in scarlet attire. The Cross-bearer entered followed by nobles carrying the Great Seal and the Cardinal's Hat on cushions, and the ushers came after, shouting, ' Make way for my Lord's Grace.' As we bowed that superb prelate sailed in, smelling his orange stuffed with aromatical spices. Then came the roll of drums announcing the King. That hammering brings it back to me now. The maskers danced in, disguised as strange shepherds in cloth of gold and red satin, attended by the drummers and torch-bearers. Wolsey feigned to believe they were Ambassadors arrived from the East,

The Fall of the Cross

as if all could not recognise the boisterous King dwarfing his comrades. How the girls shrieked, simulating astonishment, when the King flung his golden mask on the ground! How jovial he was as he hugged the nearest and threw his big arm about the Cardinal's neck! Those were light-hearted days."

"Yet sour looks were visible?"

"Ferocious old Norfolk grumbled to me, 'This is feigned mirth. It was never merry in England while we had Cardinals among us.' Wolsey heard him, and whispered, 'My lord Duke, of all men in the realm, you have least cause to be offended with Cardinals, since but for me you would have no head on your shoulders.' Norfolk shrank as he had not done when the Scots surged on the hill-top at Flodden and swooped in a torrent of multitudinous banners."

Defender of the Faith

"Yet his words were the rumbling of a storm in the distance."

"And the Cardinal has gone down in the storm. How still the night is! I think thunder is coming. Did you hear of the vision in the Magical Mirror?"

"No," replied Aske.

"I saw it that night. Wolsey, radiant at Norfolk's discomfiture, knelt to the King and said, 'Illustrious golden shepherd of England, a terrible wizard, Augustine Ciarpella, arrived from Venice to-day. Would you honour him by testing his craft?' 'I never dabble in Black Art,' said the King. 'This is white witchcraft,' said the Cardinal, smiling. 'The wizard says he can show your future Queen's likeness in his Magical Mirror.' 'Perilous skill!' cried the King, roaring a laugh. 'You should be glad her Majesty is safe at her prayers. Come

The Fall of the Cross

with me, Harry,' said he, flinging his
left arm round my neck, 'I dare not
face the Devil alone.' With that the
red tapestry at the back of the Cardinal's
dais was lifted and we saw a dim passage. As we went into it the tapestry
fell behind us and we stood in the dark.
There was a sad whisper of music, and
I felt his arm shake. Then a blur of
red light glimmered before us. As it
spread I could see it float in a glass. I
heard him pant as it flushed a vision of a
young girl all in white, carrying a bunch
of red roses. There she seemed watching
him. It was Mistress Anne's likeness."

"Mistress Anne Bullen?" said Aske.

"What are those sparks in the trees?"

"The lights of Cawood."

"I 'll take my men into the Castle
and let the others surround it. Let us
pause till they come up."

Defender of the Faith

When the Castle was surrounded a trumpet was blown and a torch appeared at a grating. Then the big door was opened by an elderly porter. The Earl ordered his gentlemen to bring in his troopers. Questioning the porter, he found the Cardinal was at supper with a chaplain and Doctor Augustine in a parlour above. So he went up the winding stairs, and Aske followed him.

The Cardinal was at the top of the stairs. Clad in red, he stood leaning on his tall silver Cross. Light from behind him shone on it, but left his face in a shadow. Seeing them, he started, and then held out his hand.

"My lord," he said softly, "you are most heartily welcome. Though I have often desired to see you here in my house, yet you would have sent me word of your coming if you had

The Fall of the Cross

loved me as I do you. Then I might have received you according to your honour and mine."

Northumberland took off his steel cap and knelt and kissed the Cardinal's ring.

"You too, Master Aske?" said the Cardinal as Northumberland rose. "So my kind friends remember me in the days of my poverty? I am sorry it is a Friday. I fear there is no fish in the house. You shall have such cheer as I am able to make you." Then he turned, peering through a loop on his left.

"My lord," he went on, "I see you recall the precepts I gave when you lived with me in your youth. You cherish your father's old servants. You have a great number with you. Surely you do well and nobly, like a wise gentleman, for these will be faithful and glad to see you prosper in honour."

Northumberland hung his head without answering.

"Come with me, my friends," said the Cardinal, leading the way into a small tapestried room lit by a couple of candles on a table and by a glimmering fire. A stout little friar with an inquisitive face stood by the hearth.

"There is my supper," said the Cardinal, smiling; "roast apples, you see. You and I have been glad at other fare, my good lord. This is my chaplain, Friar Antony Anderton." Leaning the Cross against the smirched tapestry by the head of the table, he took out a handkerchief and pressed it to his forehead and gazed at it. "The bleeding has stopped," he went on. "It was an ill omen. My lord, your trumpeter

The Fall of the Cross

frightened us. I was sitting here while Augustine stood on my left, and the Cross was leant there. Starting at the clang, he tripped over the Cross: it fell on me and wounded my forehead. Do you remember the prophecy

> ' When the Dun Cow rideth the Bull,
> Then, priest, beware thy skull ' ? "

Said Northumberland, " It is an old meaningless rhyme."

" These prophecies are tricks of the Devil and enlighten us tardily. The Dun Cow is in the arms of the Earls of Richmond; so it stands for the King."

" Ah," said the Friar, shaking his head, . " the Black Bull is the crest of the Bullens."

" God help us ! " sighed the Cardinal, sitting at the head of the table. " I sent Augustine to see who was coming; but

15

Defender of the Faith

he did not return. Be seated, my good lord," he said, pointing to the chair on his right. As the Earl took it he went on: " Let your trunk be brought up. My bedroom shall be yours while you stay with me. Plain though it is, I can give you no better in this ruinous house. There is a good fire in it. You must be chilled by your journey. Indeed, you look pale."

" More than friendship brings me here," said Northumberland.

" I shall count you still as a friend even if you have forgotten old love."

" I come in reluctance."

" And you, Master Aske?"

" I am unwilling also," said Aske.

" My enemies are skilled in afflicting me," said the Cardinal. "·What is your errand?"

Said the Earl, " It is private."

The Fall of the Cross

"Antony, leave me with my friends," said the Cardinal. Rising as the Friar went out, he said, "What sends you here so late?"

Said Aske, "His Majesty made me bring a deed for your signature."

"Is that all?"

Going forward to the Cardinal's left, Aske took out a small box bound in green velvet and barred with silver and gold. Laying it on the table, he opened it. The Cardinal took a parchment out of the box. Then he sighed and flung it down on the table.

"Tell me what it is," he said softly; "my eyes are dimmed by old age or weakened by effeminate tears."

Said Aske, "It is a conveyance."

"I have signed many recently."

"It is the King's pleasure to have your house at Westminster."

Defender of the Faith

"I hold it as Archbishop of York," said the Cardinal, reddening. "You are renowned as a lawyer. Tell me, can I give it away?"

"The judges say you can."

"And you?"

"I am not a Judge."

"What would you do in my place?"

"Nor am I a Cardinal."

"But you are a gentleman, and you would refuse. Ah, well! you are young; but I am broken by years. I have spent the best of my time in his Majesty's service, neither shunning pains nor endeavouring anything but only to please him. Is that the offence for which I am deprived of all my goods in my age? It little becomes the magnanimity of a King to condemn an ancient servant unheard and inflict on him a punishment more horrid than death. What man is so base-

The Fall of the Cross

minded that he had not rather perish a thousand times than behold a thousand men who have served him abandoned to want? For many years I have stood next to the King, great in his favour. Must I beg my bread now at the doors? Well, well! he that has nothing should be glad of a trifle, be it never so little. How shall I contend with the King? I ought to be thankful if I am let die in peace. Tell his Majesty I acknowledge my all to be derived from his bounty, and think it good reason that he should revoke his gifts if he has found me unworthy. Why should I speak of all I have when nothing is left? It is my privilege to supply him with palaces. Tell him I acknowledge my guilt. Heaven knows what it is! I make short work with you. I confess it beforehand. The combined envy of malignant adversaries may be satisfied so. A weary old man implores pardon for an ignorant crime. How shall I contend with the King?" Turning to the mantelpiece and taking a pen from an ink-bottle, he sank in his chair. Pausing as he was going to sign, he looked up at Aske. "Say to him, too," he went on, "I would have him remember there is Heaven and Hell." Signing the deed, he flung the pen on the rushes. Leaning back, he appeared suddenly aged.

Northumberland's haughty and thin face was sorrowful as he looked at the Cardinal and saw how much he had changed. Then turning to Aske, he saw him stare at the Cross while his cold scholarly face was troubled as if he was irresolute.

"My lord," said the Cardinal, "when you accompany the King in my house,

The Fall of the Cross

remember the fate of its original owner.
God has justly rewarded me for neglect-
ing my due service to Him and wholly
applying myself to his Majesty's pleasure. Woe is me! Wretch and sot that
I am, who have been ungrateful to the
King of kings! If I had served God as
diligently as I have done the King, he
would not have given me over in my
grey hairs. Is the King well?"

"I have been far from Court," said
Northumberland.

"Well and merry," said Aske, turning
and looking down at the Cardinal.

"I am glad of it," said the Cardinal
slowly. "For my part, I know death is
at hand. I have been troubled by fever
since I took a white medicine given me
by Doctor Augustine. This threatens
death or a worse evil — insanity. Mo-
mentarily I look for the hour when God

Defender of the Faith

will deliver my 'sinful soul from its loathsome prison, my body." Pausing, he
looked down at the deed. "This is just,"
he went on. "I taught His Majesty
how to plunder the Church. I meant to
reform it by annihilating irregular monasteries ; but I let the King take their
goods. I have brought ruin on the
Church — God forgive me!"

Aske raised his right hand. Northumberland rose and touched the Cardinal's
shoulder.

"My lord," he said faintly, "I arrest
you of Treason."

CHAPTER II

THE Cardinal sprang up, staggering against the tapestry and clutching the Cross with his left hand as he looked at Northumberland. The Earl folded his arms, returning the gaze.

" By what authority? " said the Cardinal.

" By the King's," said Northumberland.

" Where is your warrant? Let me see it."

" I have none."

" Then, my lord," said the Cardinal, putting the Cross between them, " I 'll not obey your arrest. Between your predecessors and mine there was contention. You said you were not here as my

23

Defender of the Faith

friend. You come as an Earl of Northumberland to conquer an Archbishop of
York. But you have come vainly.
Yorkshire will rise in arms in my cause.
That sword was my gift. Draw it against
me. Though Wolsey might bend under
a pupil's ingratitude, this Cross is the
token that the Archbishop of York defies
the Earl of Northumberland."

The Earl was going to answer; but
stopped himself, turning away.

"My lord and I are sad instruments
of your enemies' triumph," said Aske.
"Look out of that window — no, the
night is dark; but if there was a moon
you would find the Castle beleaguered.
My lord's men are inside; but others
belt it with steel. Four thousand men at
least — "

"Against one?" said the Cardinal.

Then he put the Cross back, and sat

The Fall of the Cross

down.   There was a scuffle outside, and
the door was flung open.

"Go in, or I'll make you," cried a
harsh voice.   Then Kingston appeared,
shoving a corpulent man disguised in a
grey cloak and hood.

" Master Kingston," said the Cardinal,
flushing and slapping his thigh, "the
Constable of the Tower!"

" And Captain of the Guard," replied
Kingston, kneeling, "and as such the
King sends me with your old and trusty
servants, the yeomen, to escort you to
London in all honour and by such easy
journeys as you may choose to command."

"Soft words, Master Kingston," said
the Cardinal, sighing. " I perceive other
things than you can imagine; for experi-
ence has taught me. Your comfortable
words are but of a purpose to bring me

Defender of the Faith

into a fool's paradise. Who is your prisoner?"

Rising, Kingston snatched back the grey hood and disclosed Augustine's dark face.

"There is the witness against you," said Aske.

"You have betrayed me, Augustine? Then I am doomed," said the Cardinal.

"Save me, for God's sake!" cried Augustine, falling down on his knees.

Said Kingston frigidly, "I caught him endeavouring to escape by the postern."

"Let him go," said the Cardinal.

"No," said Northumberland fiercely. "Send him to London. Tie him on a horse, and away with him!"

"I hate the sight of a horse," cried Augustine; "I'll die of fear."

"Then tie him under a horse," said Northumberland.

The Fall of the Cross

As Kingston hauled Augustine away the Earl drew himself up.

"A Northumberland might remember hereditary struggles with an Archbishop of York; but Henry Percy," he said, "is not unmindful of gratitude."

"Yet you are here, Henry Percy," said the Cardinal, rising.

"I was summoned mysteriously. Though I obeyed, I did not set out from Wharfe with a scanty following, but with a hundred of my gentlemen and a thousand retainers."

"A zealous obedience."

"At York I found an army assembled! Cromwell foresees everything, and my men were outnumbered. I have filled your house with my followers. I have accomplished my task; but now I stand at your side. Give the word, and my banner shall be flown on the ramparts. To-night the beacons shall flame. Before morning the North shall be in arms at our call."

"Harry, I wronged you," said the Cardinal, with tears in his eyes. "Here is my hand — no, not to kiss but to grasp. And you, Master Aske?" he went on.

Said Aske, "I would die gladly in the cause of the Church."

"Not in mine?"

"Now your cause is the Church's."

"It was not always so?"

Aske was silent.

"It is true," sighed the Cardinal. "Blinded by a worldly ambition, the shepherd has been false to his flock. — I have a hand for you also. I see a fair vision," he said, looking in front of him, "the Church righted by me, the King constrained to be just, the heretics and the plunderers foiled." Then he hid his

The Fall of the Cross

face in his hands. Dashing tears from his eyes, he looked at Northumberland. "It is too late," he went on. "Merciful God! It is too late. When the faithful sons of the Church rebel — as I pray they may do if this wickedness thrives — their cause shall not be stained by my guilt. If they rose for me they would endeavour to win me back the power I misused. I can but beseech God to help me. I am subject to Fortune, and I submit myself to it, ready to accept such destiny as God has provided. In a brief time I shall not be subject to Fortune."

Said Northumberland, "Yet think it over. My men shall guard you to-night. To-morrow you may be willing — "

"I am resolved."

"Pluck up your heart. The malice of your uncharitable enemies shall not prevail against you when you come to the King."

Defender of the Faith

" If I could come to him I would fear
no one. There lives no man on earth
that shall look on this face and be able to
accuse me of falsehood. My foes will
prevent my trial, destroying me by some
sinister way. My truth would vanquish
their surmised accusations. The King is
a prince of a royal courage and of a noble
heart; but rather than be balked in his
appetite he will endanger the loss of half
of his realm. I assure you I have often
knelt to him for the space of an hour, yet
could never dissuade him from a thing he
desired. When you are of his Council,
my lord, be careful what purpose you put
into his head, for he will never abandon it.
Above all things, advise him to quell this
new pernicious sect of the Lutherans, for
if they increase by his negligence he will
be driven to draw the sword to subdue
them. Remind him how the King of

The Fall of the Cross

Bohemia thought it a good game to look on while the illiterate heretics massacred the priests in his realm, till his blind mirth ended when those reprobates, strengthened by triumph, took arms against the temporal lords, and then he fought vainly and perished miserably by the judgment of God. Bid our King guard against a similar ruin."

Northumberland answered, " I mean to live retired in my home."

" God be your guide and send you good luck, even as I would myself. Heed my advice, for now I am an indifferent watcher. The sun is still in your eyes ; but I am in the shadow of death. I see how justly I have been used. To avenge an insult, I sent Buckingham to the Block in the Tower. Thus the King learnt his strength. I follow Buckingham. Because the Spaniards foiled my

wish to be Pope I sought revenge in help-
ing the King to humiliate them by divorc-
ing Queen Catherine. So I led to the
rise of my serpentine continual enemy."

" You mean Cromwell ? "

" No, I have forgiven him."

Said Aske, " He has been praised for
his constancy."

" A wily knave," said the Cardinal.
" I remember how Cavendish came on
him reading Our Lady's Matins in the
great window at Esher and crying over
his book. ' Do you weep for the Cardinal ? ' said Cavendish. — ' For myself,'
said Cromwell, ' I am like to be ruined
for serving him. An ill name once
gotten will not lightly be put away.
Now I am off to the Court, either to
make or mar.' "

" But he defended you in the Com-
mons," said Aske.

The Fall of the Cross

"To please the King. My gracious master would have seemed covetous if he had taken my wealth by force; so he wished me to surrender it all. Further, my house at Westminster and my monastic estates would have been out of his reach if I had gone to the Block. I have chilled my friends by abandoning property that belonged to the Church. There the last of it went: and the King's mercy is over. Cromwell is not to be blamed. I sinned in complying. Troubles and monumental labours have crushed me. A broken heart is too feeble to remember a grudge. I pardon Augustine, though I fear he betrayed my letter appealing for the help of the French. I trusted him foolishly."

"Trust now in the King," said Northumberland.

"I did once."

3   33

Defender of the Faith

"The King is my dearest friend, more like a brother than a sovereign to me since I was a boy."

"Ah!" said the Cardinal, "Sir Thomas More said to me, 'The King is so courteous that all believe they are loved by him, as the citizens' wives imagine Our Lady's picture in the church by the Tower smiles on them when they are praying before it. Though he favours me singularly,' said More, 'I have no cause to be proud of it, for if my head would win him a castle in France it would not remain on my shoulders.' Wise words! Yet the King is kind-hearted. Master Aske," he went on, taking a ring from his left hand, "you are going to London? Here is his likeness, painted under a ruby. Henry of England, — Defender of the Faith! The best lance and rider and archer, and the

The Fall of the Cross

comeliest man in England, built like a
tower! What tender familiar ways he
used to have with me once! How many
hours I have spent walking to and fro in
his room while that strong arm of his
was clasping my neck! How many
nights we two have paced the terrace at
Windsor, scanning the stars and dreaming
of conquest in the cause of the Church!
He was your elder brother, Harry, you
said; but he was my child, the glorious
son of my age. Take this ring, sir: he
used to send it to me when he needed my
help. I need his now. Since my disgrace he forwarded it to me in a minute
of softness. Norris brought it as I was
riding through Putney. I knelt in the
mud to receive it and sent my poor
jester in exchange, for I had no other
gift. The kind fool raged, weeping pro-
fusely, and would not go till six yeomen

carried him off. This will be eloquent.
Merciful God! Why did I never see it
before? The ruby is like a smear of
blood on his face."

"You are too wise to be disheartened
by omens," said Aske, taking the ring.

"Harry, the night we parted in the
Red Room the King saw Mistress Anne
Bullen in the Magical Mirror."

"Prophecies lead to their own fulfil-
ment," said Aske.

"Erasmus jeered at such things," said
the Cardinal. "So did More sometimes.
Yet I think he believed in them. Witty
More, with his merry and sad eyes! He
is Chancellor in my stead; but I wonder
how he will fare in his struggle with Anne
Bullen — that night-crow. Daughter of
a bad woman — 'Evil crow — evil egg,'
says the proverb. You change colour,
my lord."

The Fall of the Cross

Said Northumberland, "I have nothing to do with her."

"It would have been well for you if you had never encountered her."

"I loved her once!"

"That love may be pleasant to remember; but its danger endures. When I saw you to-night I fancied you had borne me a grudge because I parted you from her."

"You meant it kindly."

"And it was a kindness."

"Perhaps."

"Surely her conduct shows it?"

"Many speak ill of Mistress Anne," said Northumberland. "It is not probable that I should believe them."

"I do."

"You were always unjust to her."

"I was not deluded by passion."

"It was a happy illusion."

Defender of the Faith

"You saw her with the eyes of a boy," said the Cardinal angrily. "When you met, she had spent years in the corruption of Paris. You were a lad, headstrong and credulous and easily fooled."

"We would be wiser not to speak of that lady."

"Forgive me. My blood boils at the thought of her. My eyes are not indifferent yet. Still — am I wrong? My head has been confused by misfortune. I heard you were married."

"I am."

"Master Aske, I wish to speak with my lord alone for a minute."

"The King has forbidden us to see you alone," said Northumberland.

"That is unfortunate."

"I can only repeat — "

"Well, well! Master Aske is not only of unimpeachable honour, but also a dumb

38

The Fall of the Cross

oracle notorious for silence.   Briefly, then,
the King seeks a divorce from Catherine
of Arragon because she was his brother's
widow and therefore his marriage with
her was void."

" If the Pope exceeded his powers in
granting the dispensation," said Aske.

" By Canon Law," said the Cardinal,
" a betrothal is binding."

" Till a dispensation is granted," said
Aske.

" Harry, do you see your risk now ? "
said the Cardinal.

" No."

" Mistress Anne was betrothed to you
secretly."

" What ? " cried Aske.

" You dissolved that bond," said
Northumberland.

" I stopped the marriage ; but there
was no dispensation."

Defender of the Faith

"Can this be true?" said Aske sternly, as he looked at Northumberland.

"My lord Cardinal, you promised—" cried the Earl.

"To grant one, if needed."

"Well?"

"If I had heard of your coming marriage I would have warned you in time. But I had cares of my own."

"It is invalid!" said Aske.

"How could I know?" cried Northumberland.

Said the Cardinal, "If you and Mistress Anne had been constant I would not have kept you apart when you were old enough to judge the girl fairly; so I did not offer the dispensation at once. Meanwhile the betrothal was an obstacle to her wedding the King."

Said Aske, "God help the Lady Magdalen!"

The Fall of the Cross

Said the Earl, "This is nonsense, a tangle of ridiculous priestcraft!"

"You speak to a priest, my good lord," said the Cardinal.

"Are my hopes to be strangled in the net of your canonical laws? Let priests keep to their books!"

"I make allowance."

"I desire none. By this splitting of hairs you drive men to be heretics. Thus the Pope maddened the King by incomprehensible laws and dubious bought dispensations. If an act is a crime how can a dispensation be good? What need of the Pope's costly permission for an innocent act? All this trouble began because the French called the dispensation illegal. Did the Pope declare it unquestionable? No, he wavered and haggled and offered to set the King free if Queen Catherine would only consent. Was it strange that the King

wearied of truckling to a crafty Italian? I
would have done the same in his place. So
would you,—for you were always a man."

"I feel for you with all my heart," said
the Cardinal.

"Do you expect me to bring misery and
shame on my house?"

"It is a question of right and wrong,
not of the consequence."

"And I acted rightly. A boy and a
girl were betrothed; but they parted and
believed themselves free. Would she
admit the betrothal? It would ruin her.
The King does not know of it."

"Cromwell does. He was your go-
between. You wrote him a letter that
would suffice for a proof. To curry
favour with me he showed it to me, betraying your secret. No doubt, he already
planned to let her marry the King. I
remember he brought Augustine from

The Fall of the Cross

Venice and proposed the employment of the Magical Mirror. Well, I summoned you and forbade you to marry her."

"And I replied by asking her to wed me at once. It was in the Red Room — not an hour after that vision. Because she refused we quarrelled and she took back her promise. I left London that night."

"Yon think a deal of Mistress Anne," said Aske. "There is another lady concerned."

"And she is my wife."

"So she believes. Blind yourself with ignorant sophistry. But have you no care for the Lady Magdalen's honour?"

"You speak with strange passion," said Northumberland fiercely.

"I loved her vainly for years," said Aske.

"I love her also. For her sake I refuse to let anyone cast a doubt on my marriage."

Defender of the Faith

"You must tell her," said the Cardinal.

"No. She is devout and liable to be governed by priests."

"Then, Master Aske," said the Cardinal sadly, "it is your duty to warn her."

"At your peril!" said Northumberland, with his hand on his sword.

"My lord," said Aske, "honour closes my lips."

"We have been friends a long time. Before condemning my silence remember I have a daughter."

"I was unaware of it," the Cardinal said.

"A small child, but more than the world to me. Shall I make my little Cecily nameless?"

"My heart bleeds for you, Harry," said the Cardinal. "But my duty is plain. I am bound to let your wife know."

"If you dare!"

The Fall of the Cross

" Time was when the proudest noble
in England would not have dared me.
Time was when I would have answered
you roughly. Now I am infinitely tired.
If God leaves me in this world of affliction
your wife shall be aware of this secret."

" Then listen, my lord Cardinal," cried
Northumberland. " I have been eager to
draw this sword for the Church. I have
been the captain of nobles intent on an
immediate revolt. We have a hundred
thousand men at our call. I was to be
Defender of the Faith in my turn. Here
I renounce my long allegiance to Rome.
Never again shall I kneel in one of your
chapels. All this is your doing—"

" All mine," the Cardinal whispered.

" Listen in your turn, Henry Percy,"
said Aske. " You stand at the parting of
the ways. Do you wish our old friendship to be forgotten? Would you stain

a noble lady, deluding her to live as your
concubine? "

Northumberland started back and
snatched out his sword. Kingston came
in. "My lord," he began, and then drew
back in astonishment. Northumberland
thrust his sword in its sheath.

"What do you want?" he cried.

"I have sent Augustine to London as
you commanded," said Kingston, "and I
come for your orders."

"Bid my men mount," said Northumberland hoarsely. "I am about to ride
home."

"And you, sir?" said Kingston to
Aske.

"I go to London."

"And I," said the Cardinal, "I go to
rest — if I can. My sleep will soon be
quiet. To-morrow, good Master Kingston, we can set out."

The Fall of the Cross

As Kingston went Northumberland followed, but looked back from the threshold and saw Aske kneel to kiss the Cardinal's ring.

"God's blessing and mine be with you both," said the Cardinal.

BOOK II

"The Queen of the May"

CHAPTER I

NORTHUMBERLAND rode home in the dark with his ineffectual muster. As he reached Wharfe the silver tide of the dawn rippled over the black brim of the moors. The high castle was gloomy; but as he neared it a flood of light gushed on the steps and his servants came hurrying to meet him with torches.

Dismounting, he entered the firelit hall, and went up the stairs to a landing. Knocking at a door on his right, he opened it and looked into the room. There his wife was asleep, clasping his little child to

her breast. The torch on the wall of the
landing cast a gleam on her face. Steal-
ing in, he shut the door softly for fear the
light should disturb her. The gruesome
November dawn peered through the window. At the side of the bed he crossed
his arms and looked down. The girl
seemed happy and restful, and her lips
were apart: half hidden in her disordered
brown hair, his tiny daughter's cheek shone
like an apple. So he stood a long time,
and then knelt and moved the silken hair
reverently and kissed the child's forehead.
Little Cecily snuggled closer in those
sheltering arms: and his wife smiled in
her sleep as if she knew he was there.
Bending as if he would have kissed her,
he stopped, and then rested his head by
hers on the pillow. Without waking she
stirred closer to him, sighing contentedly.

Rising, he went into the opposite par-

Defender of the Faith

lour, and looked out of the front window
and saw his troopers beneath. Then he
opened the other window and heard the
Wharfe battling in the thick of the wood.
There that intricate river stormed, hidden
between precipitous banks.

Then he heard his wife mimicking a
seller of fruit. "Cherry ripe! Cherry
ripe! Who'll buy November cherries?"
she called, as she ran in, wearing a blue
cloak, and holding up their child to be
kissed.

"Ripe cherries!" she said, laughing as
he stooped to their daughter.

The child rubbed its eyes, whining
peevishly, and then smiled on Northumberland, putting its chubby arms round
his neck. Proffering her lips, she was
startled by his look and drew back; but
they were linked by the child. After
a pause she rubbed her cheek on his

shoulder, as she was accustomed to do.
He told himself they would never stand
so again.   Then he undid the child's
clinging hands.

" It is too early to wake her," he said.

" It is early to wake me," said his wife,
" Have I been dreaming ? "

" We have both dreamt," he said, turning away.

" What have I done ?   What is the
trouble ?   It is some mistake, dear," she
sobbed.   " You were in my room now:
I knew it, and woke as you left me — "

" The Lord Darcy," cried a man, opening the door at her back.

As she turned, Darcy strode in, fully
armed.

" What is this I hear ? " he stuttered.
" My Lord of Northumberland, tell me
this foul talk is untrue ! "

Northumberland faced him and then

Defender of the Faith

glanced at his wife. Quivering, she looked at old Darcy.

"What have you heard?" she said proudly as if she was accused.

"Forgive me, Madam," said square sturdy Darcy, as he saluted her: "I am glad you are present. I hear the son of my loved friend is a traitor."

"Ah!" she said.

Then she looked up at her husband as he stared at her with questioning eyes. Drawing closer to him, she stood on his left.

"You were my father's lifelong friend," said Northumberland, "and you are under my roof."

"For the last time," mumbled Darcy, "if you have betrayed us."

"If this was not my house I would answer you sword in hand, my Lord Darcy."

"The Queen of the May"

"The hangman should smash that sword and hack your spurs from your heels," stammered Darcy, while his sunburnt grim face was purple and his little eyes flamed.

Northumberland clutched his hilt and then turned to his wife and said, "I wish to be alone with my guest."

"If you are accused this is my place," she said.

Cecily had been looking on terrified, and now began crying.

"Hush, dearie, hush!" whispered Lady Northumberland.

"Before your wife, then, I accuse you of treachery," stuttered Darcy. "You have been our leader — it is time my lady should know it — you have been the chief of the lords confederate in the cause of the Church."

"I guessed it, I gloried in it," she said.

Defender of the Faith

"We were to save the Queen from dishonour, to right the Cardinal, to force King Henry to abide by the law," said Darcy. "I, who won my spurs under Henry the Seventh and helped Ferdinand to conquer the Moors, humbled myself to follow your banner. Yesterday you were ready to lead us when the Emperor's assistance was sure. There are your men!" he stammered, pointing. "Have you gathered them in our cause or against us?"

"My troops are not against you nor with you."

"I am answered," groaned Darcy. "That I should have lived to hear your father's son say it! Even now I can scarcely believe you have arrested the Cardinal."

"It is impossible!" she cried.

"You have done this for the sake of

the Concubine?" mumbled Darcy. "You are faithful to her? When we meet again, it shall be sword in hand."

As he strode out of the room she drew back.

" He must be mad," she whispered; " what can he mean? What have you to do with — with that degraded girl ? "

" That lady is my friend," said Northumberland.

" I did not think you could speak to me so," she said, wincing and crimsoning. Then she clutched the child so hard that it began crying again. " Hush, baby," she whispered as she carried it out. " You have been awakened too soon; but you have reason to cry. You are the first Percy to inherit dishonour."

That day he saw her no more, for she shut herself in her room. On the next

Defender of the Faith

evening Friar Anderton came. Northumberland, seeing him doleful and troubled, thought the Cardinal was fulfilling his
threat. The Friar recounted how Wolsey
had reached Leicester Abbey at dusk, and
had told the monks he had come to leave
his bones among them and would die at
eight in the morning, and how his words
had proved accurate. Then he was overcome by his grief and went to Lady
Northumberland.

That afternoon the Earl met her when
dinner was served in the long hall, and
found her silent and grave. The Friar
sat between them at table and seemed
perplexed for a time, but then grew
chatty again. At many following meals
he divided them, for she made him her
chaplain. At other times she would work
in her rooms or ramble out-of-doors with
her women. So she was not alone with

her husband. The Friar made no re-
mark when the Earl avoided the chapel
and ate meat during Advent. Neither
did she; but she spent more time at her
prayers.

Other things tended to embitter Northumberland. The Catholic lords shunned
him, and he saw the affection of his
people replaced by a reluctant obedience.
Of all his men one appeared as loyal as
ever; that was his foster-brother Allan
Thorne, his attendant in sports, and his
trumpeter when the troops were arrayed.
Now his rides on the moors were solitary and his way was apart. A tall girl
with grey eyes and a still and proud face
seemed the ghost of his wife.

Even little Cecily proved an apple of
discord. Because he had wronged her
he shrank from her while the Countess
sought solitude. The tiny girl seemed to

Defender of the Faith

give all her heart to her new playmate, the Friar. Northumberland suffered in losing the variable love of a child.

Cecily was a joy to the Friar, and the tasks of the household provided him with delighted astonishment. When anything was afoot he would look on with big eyes, like a rustic astounded by the ways of a city, as if he revelled in the unusual wickedness of seeing the world. An indefatigable seeker of news, he would gad in the neighbourhood and come back triumphantly with a budget of gossip.

So Northumberland learnt how More had resigned the Great Seal, and how the King had been divorced from Queen Catherine by the Archbishop of Canterbury, and had declared himself Head of the Church of England, and had been secretly married to Mistress Anne Bullen. Then the Friar brought an account of

"The Queen of the May"

Mistress Anne's coronation, telling how she had proceeded in state on the Thames from Greenwich to the Tower, and how the King had received her there amid the clamour of trumpets and the din of artillery, and how she had ridden through London gloriously on a sunny May morning, and had been crowned at Westminster while the people rejoiced.

These tidings were unwelcome to Friar Anderton. Yet he related them with a garrulous pleasure as if he delighted in picturing such stirring events. Then he began to retail gossip with sighs and much pity for poor fellows deluded by Satan as he told how More and the Bishop of Rochester had been sent to the Tower for refusing to acknowledge the King as the Head of the Church. When he had to say they had been beheaded he wept, and was sad for at least half an hour, till romping with the child, he forgot the errors of men.

On a bright morning in January the Earl was at breakfast in the chill little parlour. Lady Northumberland sat opposite him while the Friar between them held forth on the merits of the beef and the beer, for lack of something wiser to say. The child crouched on the hearth, nursing a black kitten named Michael. Cecily was now nearly five, and pretty and dark. While her parents watched her she crooned over the kitten, making believe it had sore need to be comforted.

"She cherishes that beast with a kinder passion than a woman can feel," Northumberland said as if he spoke to himself.

Then he heard his wife sigh and saw her gaze at him tenderly. Though her look froze, meeting his, yet his heart softened. A servant knocked and came

" The Queen of the May "

in with a letter and said it had been
brought by a messenger whose haste had
seemed frantic.

Northumberland rose and took the
letter uneasily and broke its ribands and
glanced at it. Flushing, he looked down
at his wife. She had been watching him;
but now she rose also and gazed out of
the front window with a weary indifference.
Then he turned to Cecily. She had been
roused from her nursing, and ran to the
Friar, saying, " Oh, Father! what can be
the matter with Michael? He looks so
miserable that I am sure he is sick."

The Friar fondled her and promised
to call a doctor at once and persuaded
her not to squeeze the kitten so tight.
As she ran back to the hearth, holding
the animal in a more cautious embrace,
Northumberland read the letter again.
Then he pitched it into the fire.

Defender of the Faith

"I am going to London," he said, looking at his wife, "I may be gone for some time."

"Indeed?" she said without turning.

For a minute he watched her with a hardening face. Then he stooped, hugging the child.

"You'll hurt Michael," she said peevishly, wriggling out of his arms. "He is dreadfully ill."

There was a thud of hoofs on the gravel, and Friar Anderton jumped up and trotted to the window, rejoicing in the unexpected excitement.

"It is Master Aske," he said eagerly.

The Earl paused irresolute.

"Father, who is Anne?" said the child.

He saw she had rescued the letter from the smouldering logs.

"'I need your help—Anne,'" she read shrilly. "Oh! how well I read, Father!"

" The Queen of the May "

she said to the Friar. " Stop him ! "
she screamed. The kitten had fled from
her clutch, and now escaped from the
room as the servant opened the door.

" Master Robert Aske ! " said the
servant.

As Cecily rushed after the kitten the
Friar pursued her, crying, " She will
tumble downstairs ! "

Lady Northumberland turned. As
Aske entered she greeted him with a
stately serenity. The Earl looked at him
as if they were strangers.

" My lord, I come with a message from
the King," said Aske slowly.

" What is it, Sir ? " said Northumberland.

" He desires you and my lady to attend
him in London."

" As prisoners ? " said Northumberland, flushing.

Defender of the Faith

" As guests," replied Aske. " Here is his letter."

As the Earl read it Aske and Lady Northumberland looked at each other.

" It is long since we roamed by Derwent Water," she whispered.

Crumpling the letter, Northumberland went out of the parlour. Going to his bedroom, he armed, and summoning Thorne, told him to make ready for travel and fetch a couple of horses. As he went down the stairs he saw his daughter below, brandishing the unfortunate kitten while the Friar was attempting to calm her.

" I have to set out at once," he said to the Friar. " I wish you would beg Master Aske to take a hundred horsemen and guard my lady if she travels to London."

" And I ? " said the Friar.

"The Queen of the May"

"You must have the kindness to give orders here in our absence."

"I am to have charge of the Castle," Friar Anderton said, lifting his plump hands in delight; "I am to take care of the child!"

Then Allan Thorne rode up to the door with a led horse, and Northumberland mounted. In the saddle he looked at the parlour window, but saw nobody there. Turning to his child, he saw her making the Friar kiss the kitten's sleek head. So he shook his reins and rode off.

Reaching London at midday on the seventh of January, he found the side of Throgmorton Street blocked by citizens and heard trumpets approaching. So he halted at the back of the crowd.

The day had an irresolute brightness.

Defender of the Faith

Cheers rang in the distance, and rose and were taken up by his neighbours as the trumpeting grew. The women waved their handkerchiefs gladly, and the men tossed their caps as the trumpeters passed, followed by red ranks of the yeomen.

Then the King came riding alone: he wore yellow silk and a short mantle of ermine and a round cap of crimson velvet with a flaunting white plume. As he lounged, managing a white horse hung with trappings of cloth-of-gold, he was nodding with a lazy good-humour. On his big horse he towered above his worshipping people. Though he was still glowing and fortunate there was a lurking uneasiness in his masterful eyes.

When the King passed and the crowd scattered and the trumpets grew far the Earl rode to Northumberland House. There he dressed in black and gave

"The Queen of the May"

orders to have everything prepared for his wife's coming. Then he went to take a boat at the Tower. The river was strong, and many seagulls were over it. More's head was on a spike on the bridge. That ghastly head had been the wisest in England. Those sockets had held grave and sweet eyes: now they glowered at the gulls while the Londoners were cheering the King.

Northumberland remembered how More had landed on those steps, while the Axe was carried before him with its blade turned to him as a sign of his doom, and how his daughter Margaret waited on her knees for his blessing, but could not quell her grief, and rose breaking through the soldiers, and clung to him, and how on the eve of his death he wrote to her, " I never liked your manner towards me better than when you kissed me last, for

Defender of the Faith

I love when daughterly love and dear charity have no leisure to look to worldly courtesy."

Then he recalled how Mistress Anne had arrived at those steps, seated in her state barge and clad in white tissue with her hair hanging loose, and preceded by fifty boats full of music and banners and a raft covered with fantastical monsters surrounding a gilt dragon that spouted wild-fire, while the trumpets clanged and the cannon crashed on the battlements and the King waited to welcome her.

Those contrasted scenes haunted him as he was rowed up the river. One moment he would see Mistress Anne, a restless and vain child and a loving trifler with hearts, and the next he would re-member More's pale and firm face, and his knack of holding his right shoulder higher than his other, and his sad little

" The Queen of the May "

jokes. So too, when the Abbey loomed
dark with the stains of centuries, a different picture came to his mind's eye, and
he saw Windsor Castle dominate the
battalions of trees, the warden of the
forest. At Westminster he went up
the trim path where he and Mistress Anne
used to dally in the Cardinal's time.
Now the roses were leafless and the yeomen of the Guard were about and the
royal banner was up. The galleries of
the Palace were empty. Revisiting the
haunts of his boyhood, he went into the
Red Room and saw Cromwell.

CHAPTER II

A BIG gilt chair stood where the Cardinal's high daïs had been. There Cromwell sat stooping, covering his mouth with his hand. With his neglected brown clothes and his ponderous ruddy face and his untidy black hair overhanging his ears he had the look of a peasant. Hearing Northumberland, he sprang up with an awkward alacrity. Now that his pinched mouth and his frosty eyes were visible, his look was transformed. Then he rubbed his coarse hands like an obsequious tradesman.

" My kind patron," he said gladly in his pleasant and deep voice as he went to the Earl, " you honour me ? "

70

"The Queen of the May"

"And find you enthroned," said Northumberland.

"Not a word of that," replied Cromwell uneasily. "I forgot myself and sat
down for a minute. Men's heads have
fallen for less. But you will not speak of
it. I remember how much I owe to your
graciousness."

"You owe much to your craft."

"Eh? The King finds me useful;
but my head is not turned. A beggar in
purple forgets himself; but you see my
homespun is brown."

"You are wise."

"You doubt me," said Cromwell as he
straddled and thrust his muscular hands
under his belt. "Well, remember my
past. Son of a Putney tradesman, driven
from home by a stepfather's malice, an
innocent prisoner, a wronged fugitive, a
vagabond abroad, servant to a foot-soldier,

Defender of the Faith

a ruffian myself for lack of easier liveli-
hood, a beggar at Frescobaldi's threshold
in Florence, then his clerk, and a slow
winner of comparative wealth, — there is
my history in a nutshell, my lord."

" I could continue it."

" Eh ? A moneylender willing to help
shiftless and thriftless nobles, then the
Cardinal's servant, now the King's secretary, able to make or mar. Well, how
can I have the pleasure of aiding
you ? "

" I did not come here to look for you."

" I am sorry for that," said Cromwell.
" You look bitter and pale. Troubled ? "

" When I ask for your pity — "

" We are all changed. Mistress Anne
— You frown — An old sore ? I had
hoped it was cured." Northumberland
was turning away, but Cromwell went
on. " Let us talk for a little."

" The Queen of the May "

" What do you want ? "

" How desolate the old Abbey seems !
No doubt, you resented being chosen to
arrest Cardinal Wolsey. You were bene-
fited, for now you are free from toothless
stuttering Darcy and other risky companions. Mistress Anne chose you. Now
there is a change ! I am the Secretary ;
but she is the Queen—or the Concubine ?
Fluttering in a gleam of the sunlight, she
forgets it is winter. When the butterfly
is draggled by rain, it shall crawl in the
mud, liable to be crunched under-foot,"
said Cromwell, stirring his heel. Looking
at the Abbey, he went on as if he was
thinking aloud, " If she basked in the
sun with everything her heart could desire
she would be innocuous. We thirst for
wine, and the gods lavish it on us as soon
as the years have soured it to vinegar.
Through many days the Concubine en-

tangled the King. Now his strength dies, and his love verges on hate."

"You speak of a lady."

"And of our mortal foe," answered Cromwell, turning to him with glittering eyes. "Though I gave her a crown, I find her arrogance and malice intolerable. Yesterday, standing there, she threatened to take my head off my shoulders. My head is not pretty; still I would be sorry to lose it. Hers is beautiful — Well!"

Northumberland was silent, remembering her beautiful face.

"An unrivalled comedian, a charming girl," Cromwell went on, "full of criminal happiness and innocent gaiety. All gaiety is innocent, as flame must be pure though it rises from the burning of filth. Vanity incarnate! an irresistible weed! Have you read that new book 'Pantagruel'? As purity would be corruption in Rabe-

"The Queen of the May"

lais, so any virtue would be a fault in the
Concubine. — Wait! A vulgar gardener
is accustomed to call a spade by its name.
Can you make a silk purse from a sow's
ear? Rather than share your supercilious
refinement, I would prostrate myself in
natural dirt, as a hog wallows in the muck
of its sty. I 'll feign to respect her. Yet
I must warn you the years have shown
other merits in that amorous child. Now
she hates readily. Often her laughter
is an ominous mirth: she may live to
find it unfortunate. The King might forgive her heresy, though he is Head of the
Church, or her siding with France, though
he would prefer to help Spain; but she
welcomes his poems with injudicious
hilarity. Mockery stings him while his
favourite jests are practical and often un-
kind. — Do you remember how the Bishop
of Rochester's cook was accused of poison-

ing, and the King had him boiled as an appropriate punishment?— Nothing can madden him as much as a slight to his poetical gifts or his theological learning. The fate of England is altered because he was first meant to be Archbishop of Canterbury. The stone thwarting the trickle guided the river to the ultimate sea."

"All these dark sayings — "

" They are dark to you, my good lord? I like you the better. I am so much alone that I am tired of intellectual company. I have been alone all my life."

"You may remain so, as far as I am concerned."

" One minute! Do you wish to know why the King sent for you? "

" Why? " said Northumberland.

" Merely because I discovered Mistress Anne summoned you. So he invited you and your wife, choosing a more public attendance. Besides, I wanted to see you — ''

The Earl broke in impatiently, "What has become of the letter I wrote you ? "

" A letter ? "

" Have you destroyed it ? "

" If you sent me one I must have kept it."

" Give it back to me."

" I shall look for it gladly."

" I insist."

" Why trouble about it ? The Cardinal dissolved the betrothal and granted the necessary dispensation, of course."

" He granted none."

" Eh ? "

" For your own sake — "

" My toil is expended for the good of the world. You sneer, my lord. Yet it is true. I am incapable of bragging or cringing. You were impatient when I

Defender of the Faith

talked of my history; but I spoke with a purpose. Remembering how much I have suffered, you may believe I am labouring to right the oppressed. My methods are alien, for I learnt them in Italy. Is Machiavelli's wisdom unfit for commodious and temperate England? — I have an offer to make. Your marriage is void? You are lucky. Lord! to see how a man will barter his prime for the transitory illusions of love, masking his nature and mincing to please some idiotical girl! The King trades his birthright for the sport of lascivious children. These meddlesome women! I am glad I am elderly, out of reach of their prayers and fond flickerings."

"Room for the Queen!" cried an usher.

Clad in a long mantle of ermine, the Queen came in proudly. Seeing North-

"The Queen of the May"

umberland, she started and blushed holding out her hands to him joyfully. As he grew pale and stepped forward trumpets began announcing the King. That music divided them, and they were suddenly still. Then she shunned his eyes and saw Cromwell. Drawing back her left hand, she proffered the other to Northumberland coldly.

"You are welcome, my good lord," she said carelessly.

As he knelt kissing her hand she glanced at Cromwell with a flash of defiance; but it left him unmoved. Then as Northumberland rose, her hazel eyes were mocking and sweet. Looking at him, she flung back her mantle, disclosing a rich purple dress with wide sleeves, and clasped her jewelled fingers demurely.

"You find me changed?" she asked.

Defender of the Faith

"Not much, Madam," he answered, wondering what was the difference he felt, for though she appeared no older and her dark hair hung down in her habitual fashion, yet she seemed unfamiliar.

"What brings you to London?" she asked quickly. "Why did you abandon us? Do you mean to stay now? Come over here. You have to earn my forgiveness for this cruel desertion."

Crossing the room with a languid grace, she took the gilt chair at the top of the table.

"Now what can you say to heal my broken heart?" she asked. "Kneel, my loving subject, and justify your barbarous acts. Too stubborn?" she went on, laughing, as he stood on her left. "How well I remember your lofty ways! But the Queen gives a command." Then she whispered, "Anne begs it, dear."

"The Queen of the May"

Northumberland knelt, bowing his head.

"You used to be ready to kneel, Harry," she whispered, fondling his hair. Though her voice was loving, her eyes were bitter as they dwelt upon Cromwell.

Said Northumberland, "Let me rise, Madam."

"Call me Anne, and I may, dear," she whispered with her eyes on her enemy.

"Let me rise, Anne," he whispered.

"Rise," she said, leaning back. "I can still master you," she went on, smiling, and fingering the gold chain on her neck. "Yes, you are welcome. The Queen of England is glad to have her friends at her side. The more the merrier, though I have thousands while my enemies are few and short-lived. They will soon be fewer." With that she began laughing again.

"Who are they?"

Defender of the Faith

"You look dangerous. I'll not ask you to hurt them : they are too insignificant. I snap my fingers at them all," she said merrily, suiting the action to the word. "If I wave my hand thus they are gone. Would you believe anyone could be hostile to me? I'll tell you the name of my most perilous enemy. He will not vex me much longer; so you ought to observe him. Bend that proud head of yours — I'll whisper it, as he is not far."

"Madam, the King comes," said Cromwell.

Turning white, she leapt up, as a gruff voice began singing :

> "Le temps s'en va,
> Le temps s'en va, ma dame."

"He must not find you here," she cried, trembling. Then she lifted the

" The Queen of the May "

tapestry at her side and gasped, ".There
is a hidden door. Go out by it, for God's
sake."

" Not I," said Northumberland.

" For my sake," she whispered.

" It is necessary," said Cromwell.

Crossing the room, he went into the
passage behind the arras.

" This way," he went on, " I 'll open
the door."

Northumberland hesitated, and went
after him as the King sauntered in, hum-
ming,

" Le temps s'en va,
   Le temps s'en va, ma dame.
   La! Le temps non, mais nous nous en allons."

" Ha! Anne!" said the King as he
swaggered into the room with his rolling
stride. " You were wrong to stop in. It
was pleasant out in the sun."

Defender of the Faith

" I was — I was not very well," she said, looking at him and trying to see whether he had noticed her arranging the curtain.

" You never are now," he said fretfully.

Then as he lolled in the gilt chair he frowned at her, nearly closing his eyes. Meanwhile Cromwell went up the steps in the dark passage, and opening a secret door, passed through it, and shut it again. The Earl found it locked. While he shook it he heard Cromwell retreating.

" My health does not matter now," said the Queen, shrugging, as she stood on the King's right. " Others are strong."

" Who ? " the king asked.

" That white doll, Jane Seymour, — and that saucy babe, Catherine Howard."

" You are jealous," he said, smiling complacently. " I am too lazy to wrangle," he

" The Queen of the May "

went on, leaning back, shutting his eyes drowsily and stretching his arms.

At that moment Northumberland lifted the curtain angrily, as if he was entering. With a glance at the King, she clasped her hands, and looked at Northumberland as if she was begging for life. Irresolute, he turned from her eyes; and then saw the door at the end of the room opening and his wife coming in. Guided by his look, the Queen saw Lady Northumberland draw back on the threshold. For some seconds they stood so. Then Lady Northumberland turned and went out. The Earl looked again at the Queen, and drew back and let the tapestry fall.

With a malicious triumph in her eyes, the Queen said, " I 'll not vex you."

" You had better not," the King growled with good-humour, as he looked up.

Defender of the Faith

"Your eyes are red, baby," he went on, as he pulled her on his knee. "You have been crying again."

"I have been sleepless."

"Why?"

"Thinking of you."

"How could you be better employed?" he said, fondling her neck. "I'll forgive that,—but no tears, mind you! Catherine was always in tears. I chose you as a companion in happiness. While I was young I could be merry in spite of a woman's peevishness. Wolsey encouraged me to make the most of my youth while he bore the burden of state — disinterested advice! When I found youth had passed I saw my life ridden by priests and frittered in the rejoicings of fools. It was time to be free, and a King. And I am. A little neck!" he muttered, closing his hand on it.

"The Queen of the May"

"You choke me," she gasped.

Still he throttled her. Then he flung her off.

"There — be warned," he said grimly.

Gasping, she rubbed the tears from her eyes.

"No tears," he repeated.

"Then grow gradually stern," she sobbed, "change to me slowly. When I am accustomed to harshness I'll bear it without crying; but now if you are angry I think my sun is obscured by a momentary cloud, and I weep."

"I am not angry," he said. "A good girl — a loving child, I am sure. You are sunny again. Laugh, baby. That is right. While you laugh you can do anything with me."

"Then I shall laugh for ever."

"I want no other music."

"Once you liked my singing."

Defender of the Faith

"And I do still. Laugh and sing,
and I am wax in your hands."

"What shall I sing, sweetheart?"

"None of those doleful songs of yours.
Tell me of happiness."

"Here is one I made for you."
Then she sang,

> "There she stood with morning face,
> Singing in the market-place,
> Moulded to be Queen of all:
> Cowslips were her coronal."

The King laughed, and joined her at
the top of his voice,

> "King Cophetua forsook
> His high throne and royal look:
> 'Will you be my Queen,' he said,
> 'And no more a beggarmaid?'"

"And I said 'yes,'" she whispered,
"golden Cophetua."

"And King Cophetua was a beggar

"The Queen of the May"

for the rest of his days," he said, putting his big arm round her waist.

" What did he beg? " said she, smiling.

" Guess."

" I do," she said, kissing him.

" A dainty witch," he said, hugging her.

" Ah! that reminds me! " she sighed as she leant her cheek against his.

" I might have known you wanted something," he grumbled. " Yet I have changed the cowslip-crown into gold."

" Fairy-gold changes into cowslips again."

" Before it does, ask what you like."

" My King has outdone his girl's extravagant dreams."

" The power to do that is the recompense of the cares of a King."

" I want nothing now but your happiness."

Defender of the Faith

"Well, I am happy now," he said, kissing her.

"But your bliss lacks its crown, an heir," she whispered, "a little son for us both."

"True," he sighed, letting her go.

"When you called me a witch," she said, "I remembered how Augustine the Wizard had consulted the stars."

"Where?" he said anxiously.

"At Kimbolton."

"What does he say?"

"The Lady Catherine of Arragon's star and mine are opposed."

"I could have told him that."

"One of us must die before long. And he discovered I never can have a son while she lives."

"This is your desire!" he said savagely. "Her head as a toy? It was More's last time. You were the cause of that man's death, daughter of Herodias!"

"And he was a traitor," she answered. "There is a prophecy — "

"What is it?"

"The Rose Decorate of England shall be slain in his mother's womb."

"That has been interpreted. I am the Rose Decorate, and the Church is my mother. I am to be killed by the priests. I shall have killed some of them first."

"Our son would be another Rose Decorate. Well, I ought to have known my danger would be nothing to you compared with the peril of offending the Spaniards."

"Ha!" he said, flushing, "yet I have proved how little I mind them."

"No," she said, "you flinch from the proof."

Defender of the Faith

" You are bold."

" In your cause.   Send Catherine of Arragon and her bastard to the doom they
have earned.   You have lopped the boughs
of rebellion.   Lay the axe to its roots.   I
am utterly shamed when the world scorns
you for sparing them.   So great a King,
and a coward shuddering from the anger
of Spain ! "

" You try my forbearance."

" Fearlessly.   I am not blind enough to
think you are merciful for the sake of old
service.   Have I rendered none?   You
are as indebted to me as a man can be to
a woman.   If you are wealthy to-day who
made you resolute when you inclined to
let the monks fatten on the gold they
had wrested from the people by craft?
I saved you from an incestuous union.   Is
this your love for me?   Catherine of
Arragon is your Queen, after all.   I?

"The Queen of the May"

What am I? Your plaything, your concubine?"

"No man dare say it!" he cried.

"All the world does. Your grovelling courtiers whisper it to one another with sneers. Am I a slut from the ditches? Am I less noble than a Princess of Arragon? I have the hot blood of Ormond: I am a daughter of the Howards, your Majesty. Or do you slight me because my beauty is less than that withered treacherous foreigner's? Yet you used to praise it. Ah! if she is the fairer, I am the more loving. What did you ever find in her eyes but sanctimonious contempt? Look now in mine."

"Catherine shall bend or break," he cried, striking the table. "I can no longer endure the alarm and trouble she causes."

As she clung to him, he took her

small face in his hands, and stared into her passionate eyes.

"I see a King's likeness in these magical mirrors," he said.

"Because you are peeping out of my heart."

"If only I was sure of it!"

"If you could see yourself with my eyes you would not doubt it. If they shine it is because they are flooded by the light of my sun. I am like the ruby ring you have there."

"A rich jewel."

"Made valuable by enshrining the King. When I am waking you thrill me: and you master my dreams. Day and night my ears hold your voice as a shell echoes the ocean."

"A pink elaborate shell," he said, pulling her ear, "a hoarse voice to remember."

"The ocean is gruff," she said, smiling.

"The Queen of the May"

"Your voice is a soldierly music that should be accompanied by the rumble of drums."

"I am a maimed soldier. Cophetua is fallen," he muttered. "I am twice your age, and afflicted with a loathsome and incurable illness. — God help me! I should be thinking of death." With that he thrust her away.

"You chose me to share pleasure," she said. "You only wanted me to smile and be sweet when we drifted on the silvery Thames or lingered in gardens where the nightingales sang. My husband, keep me as a companion in suffering."

"A man suffers and dies alone."

"Not alone when he is loved by his wife."

"In a short time this body will rot below the feet of the living. Another will sit here in my stead. You will be happy and laughing in another's embrace."

Defender of the Faith

"Do you know me so little?" she sobbed.

"No tears!" he said angrily. "The King can die unwept. Life would be bearable if hearts could be read; or would that make the world Hell? Did you — how many did you love before meeting me?"

"You hurt me, dear," she said, crying.

"I am not blaming you. How could any one see that little face without loving it? Wherever you go you must be haunted by worship. That soft heart must have been melted in its ignorant youth. Stop crying, baby: I hate to see it. I'll not be angry, dear. I might have blamed you for a premature coldness. Frost is untimely in the days of Spring. God made my sweetheart kind. I am not doubting your honour, nor suggest-

ing you were in any way bound — I
know you too well — I speak of infantile
trifles, the groping in the unknown and
desired path of Love natural to the heart
of a child."

Still she cried bitterly, with her face in
her hands.

" I 'll not ask you his name," he said.
" You must have known a brief fancy.   I
tell you I am sure of it, baby.   I 'll trust
you all the more if you own it."

" I thought you trusted me fully."

" So I do, so I do," he said soothingly.
" You imagined you loved a fortunate
boy?   It was all long ago, and he is married, no doubt, as you are.   Still bashful?
Come to your husband, dear.   Give him a
kiss — that will be your only avowal.
We 'll say no more about it."

As he held out his arms she wavered
towards him, and then stopped.

Defender of the Faith

" I have told you often," she sobbed,
" I have loved nobody."

" Love's tender perjury," he said, smiling, as he let his arms drop.

" You swore the same to me."

" Did I ? I have sworn it to many."

" But I believed it," she sobbed.

" A pretty simpleton."

Taking heart, seeing his good humour,
she whispered, " When I was very young,
I fancied I loved — "

" Ha ! " he said, frowning.

" My father and mother," she said,
shaking with fear.

" You play with me, minx," he said,
smiling.

" But I never thought I cared for anyone else."

All this time Northumberland listened against his will in the passage. Now
the door at his back was opened, and he

" The Queen of the May "

sprang up the steps, expecting to find Cromwell, and so came on his wife. For a minute she looked at him sadly without any reproach. Then he turned, strode down the steps, tore back the arras, and confronted the King.

CHAPTER III

"I SWEAR you are the first I have loved,"
the Queen was saying as Northumberland entered.

"Guards!" shouted the King, leaping
up and clutching his dagger.

"I trusted you to go," she whispered,
shuddering, with her eyes on Northumberland.

As the Earl knelt the guards came
running in. The King waved his hand,
and they huddled out of the room.

"Ha! my friend Harry," he said
lazily as he sat down, "you came
abruptly; but I know it is because you
are eager after long separation." Then
he looked at her and smiled tenderly

with his eyes nearly shut. " What were
you saying, sweetheart ? " he asked.

She turned, clutching a chair.

" Sit down," he went on. " You are
white. It is tiring to act comedies, Anne.
— You were in the hidden passage ? " he
said, throwing his arm round the Earl's
neck. " I saw her Majesty arranging the
tapestry ; but I believed the secret door
would be open. You heard me speak
of my sickness ? I do not wish that
slight complaint to be known. I spoke
of it, since a husband should keep nothing from his affectionate companion in
suffering. Three may keep counsel if
two be away. If I thought my cap knew
my counsel I would throw it into the
fire. You understand ? Rise. I have
missed you," he went on, lounging as
Northumberland rose. " Hunting has not
been the same without you : and none

Defender of the Faith

of my Court can draw the bow as you
used. I rode and shot better than you
did; but I like to have rivals." Then
he paused, chuckling. " So you have
been living in the North with your
wife? — Happy he who never saw a
King and whom a King never saw.
But should a King be forsaken by his
brother in the hour of his need? "

" I did not know you had need of
me," said Northumberland, with his eyes
on the ground.

" The truth is, I am old, too un-
wieldy for dances — a little testy, perhaps. Hunting — I have given that up.
Where can I find a hunter that can
carry me now? Archery too — I have
hung my bow on the wall. It is too
big for you degenerate lads. Now my
hand is unsteady. Yet it can still hold
a sceptre, a golden toy for my age.

"The Queen of the May"

Yes, Harry, you and Norris abandon me to herd with the young. Norris passes his days in dancing and making love — the young reprobate! Well, I did the same once. Now I sit solitary and envy his naughtiness, and laugh while he frolics on the brink of a precipice." Laughing, he put his hands on his sides.

Northumberland stood with crossed arms, while the Queen leant on the table.

"You, Norris, and I," the King went on, "'The Three Harrys' — two of them boys, and the third stubbornly forgetful of Time — what revels we had! Lord! what gluttons we were, and how we tossed off the bumpers till the dawn was aghast, and how we reeled back from Northumberland House through the twilit streets, shouting old ballads, making the fat citizens turn on their

Defender of the Faith

pillows and say, 'There goes hearty
King Hal!' and how we would mount
then and ride under the thick woods of
Hampstead in the fresh hours, the delicious prime of the morning! I shall
never sing again in the streets, hugging
your necks. No more a glutton — Pleasure is not good for my health — "

Then an usher opened the door, saying,
"Sir Henry Norris craves an audience,
your Majesty."

"I sent him for news of the Lady
Catherine," said the King as the Queen
rose. "Bid him come up. Ha! you are
yourself again, sweetheart. That name is
medicinal. Why do you avoid looking
at Harry? Quarrelled? Here!" he
went on, springing up and gripping her
shoulder, "Kiss and be friends!"

With that, he thrust her into Northumberland's arms. The Earl shrank,

and she shuddered, and then proffered
her face to him. As he stooped, kissing
her forehead, the King said, " Be kind
to her when I am gone, Harry."

Norris, coming in, started angrily as
he saw that embrace : his crimson clothes
were bespattered.

" You look hot," said the King to
him. " You have ridden hard ? What
news from Kimbolton ? "

" Grave tidings," said Norris, approaching him and kissing his hand.

" What are they ? " the Queen asked
breathlessly.

" The Lady Catherine is dead," answered Norris. As he rose, turning to
her, his reckless young face was haggard,
and his eyes were reproachful.

" At last ! " she cried gladly.

" Dead ! " the King muttered. " Praise
be to God ! Now the alliance of Rome

Defender of the Faith

and France and Spain will be broken. We are out of danger of war. We 'll give the French a lesson, and teach them how to trifle with us. This removes all grounds of difference with the Emperor. — Good!"

"How did she die?" whispered the Queen.

Said Norris, "Of some mysterious disease."

The King stooped and peered at her. Northumberland also looked at her, and she tossed her head scornfully.

"She was attended by a doctor?" she said, as if she defied them.

"By Augustine," said Norris, turning away.

"Ha!" said the King.

"Did she complain?" she asked, trembling and looking down. "Did she — did she write any letter?"

"The Queen of the May"

"Here is one for his Majesty," said Norris, bending his knee.

The King took the letter and fumbled with its seal, watching the Queen. Then he flung it on the table.

"She troubled me enough in her lifetime," he said, sitting down. "A spiteful and unforgiving woman she was. Many a time has she annoyed me with letters. This is the last. I have a foreboding it would vex me again. Why should I read it? I have done with her. I am free. Here am I in council with those who love me best. Norris, what do you say? Shall I destroy it unread?"

"I would," said Norris.

"One vote," said the King, with a nod. "And you?" he went on, as he peered at Northumberland.

"It may hold her last requests," said the Earl. "I would read it."

Defender of the Faith

The Queen glanced at him fiercely; and he stared at her, wondering. Now he appreciated the change in her looks: her pretty and demure mouth had become hard and her red lips thicker and her dimpled chin prominent and her bold hazel eyes cynical and haunted by care.

"And you," said the King. "What would you do?"

"This," she answered, snatching the letter and tearing it. "That rebel's conspiracies are over at last."

"You are too hasty," he said. "Harry, I have been deprived of your counsel: I'll not slight it so soon. Take the letter and read it out."

As Northumberland hesitated Norris stretched out his hand; but the King said, "Leave it to him."

Northumberland took it irresolutely.

"Break the seal," said the King.

" The Queen of the May "

" Undo the riband — that is right. Unfold the bits. Spread them there. Good ! "

As Northumberland stooped the Queen leant on the gilt chair, watching him with feverish eyes.

" ' The hour of my death now approaching,' " he read, " ' I cannot choose but out of the love I bear you advise you of your soul's health, which you ought to prefer before all considerations of the world or flesh whatsoever — ' "

" True," said the King, nodding.

" ' — for which yet you have cast me into many calamities and yourself into many troubles.' "

" Very true ! " said the King.

" ' But I forgive you all and pray God to do so likewise,' " Northumberland read. Then he paused and went on, " ' For the rest I commend to you Mary, our daughter, beseeching you to be a good father to her, as I have always desired.' "

" Ha!" said the King, shutting his eyes.

" ' I must entreat you also to respect my maids, and give them in marriage, which is not much, they being but three; and to all my other servants a year's pay besides their due, lest they should be unprovided. Lastly, I make this vow that my eyes desire you above all things. Farewell.' "

" Is that all?" said the Queen, drawing a breath.

Without facing her, Northumberland crumpled the torn bits in his hand.

" Poor Kate!" said the King. " Those haughty eyes are blind. I wish I had visited her. I did not think she was dying. The Court shall go into mourning," he went on as he stood. " The Lady Catherine shall be buried with the

"The Queen of the May"

honour befitting a Princess of Arragon. Madam, you are rosy again. That is right. Life is too short to be squandered on avoidable care. Norris, call Cromwell. — Ha! You grow white, dear? — I 'll see him apart. I 'll be back soon, perhaps before I am wanted. I must send someone to condole with the Emperor. This news will alter the world. Would you like to go to Spain, Norris? I see you would not. Stop where you are happy and safe. Leave ambition to men unlucky in love. Cromwell and I are elderly, and toil is the pastime of our monotonous days. We are killjoys, and the thought of us banishes the fugitive roses from delicate cheeks. That is true?" he asked, pinching her.

"You hurt me," she said.

"I am still able to make a velvety cheek redden," said he. "Comfort her

for my cruelty, boys. Swear beauty is
eternal. Tell her a fair woman is out of
reach of the Law, for the King shall be
her footstool."

So he went out with a lagging step,
muttering, " Poor Kate ! How time slips
away !

'La ! Le temps non, mais nous nous en allons.'"

Northumberland stooped, and put the
letter into the fire.

As the bits flared, she said breathlessly,
" Why — why did you burn it ? "

" Madam, may I withdraw ? " he said
coldly, without meeting her eyes.

" The King ordered you to stop."

" You did right," said Norris, touching
his shoulder. " If the King had not
checked me I would have burnt it
unread."

" The Queen of the May "

" Why ? " said Northumberland, with a look of suspicion.

As Norris flushed and drew back she said with a laugh, " Because he is my friend. You advised — "

" I was mistaken."

" You were my friend once," she said slowly, " so I summoned you, thinking I could count on your help. I can find willing assistance."

Then she held her hand out to Norris. As he knelt kissing it she fondled his light curls with her other and looked at Northumberland with a tender reproach.

" Time tries all," she said softly. " Yet, my lord, I suspect you like me more than you think. What do you say ? " she asked Norris, taking his arm as he rose. " Has my lord forgotten my spells ? "

Defender of the Faith

"That is impossible," cried Norris adoringly.

"Flatterer!" she said with languishing eyes. "But honestly?"

"Let him speak for himself."

"I ask you."

"I can only judge by his acts," said Norris pettishly.

"Jealous? Foolish boy!" she said, laughing. "Well, I'll copy you. His acts are as kind as his words used to be once."

"Those words must have proved an undesirable kindness," said Norris, frowning.

"I used to love them," she answered. "I say your acts are tender, my lord, because you skipped something when you were reading that letter. I saw it — "

"So did the King," said Norris.

"God forbid!" she cried, drawing away from him.

"The Queen of the May"

"That is," said Norris as if he repented alarming her, "my lord delayed long enough to rouse his suspicion."

"But did he notice? I was not looking."

"How can anyone tell what the King sees?"

"What a coward you are!" she said, laughing. "Never frown at me! I have told you a hundred times he sees nothing."

"Well, I hope you are right."

"From the way you talk, one would fancy we had something to hide. You will disgust my good Lord of Northumberland, that mirror of loyalty. It is your turn to look angry," she said to the Earl. "Never mind what I say. You know I am mischievous. Jesting apart, I thank you for destroying the letter. I fear the King will resent your burning it. You are not afraid? Take example by him," she went on, smiling at Norris. "So a man should stand crossing his arms instead of imagining danger. The King is dull and sleepy and old. You should see how puzzled he looks when my talk is too rapid for his labouring wits. You make him out a grim morose tyrant. Though I am weak, I love peril. If I was a man and as big as you are, I'd blush — "

"With your Majesty's leave," Norris broke in, "I shall withdraw."

"With all his dullness the King has foresight. If he had not ordered you both to stay I would be left to myself. I'll not tease you. It is a shame, and frowns make you so ugly. There," she said, drawing a finger across his forehead caressingly, "now the wrinkles have faded."

As Norris kissed her hand passion-

ately she said to Northumberland, " I
am afraid to smooth yours : they look
permanent. Your forehead was like a
girl's, I remember. Tell me what you
passed over. You know how curious I
am."

" I had rather not," he replied.

"I insist, — I mean I beg it as a favour," she said, clasping her hands.

The Earl glanced at Norris.

" He is in all my secrets," she said,
" or thinks he is."

" Am I wrong ? " said Norris.

" Well, you are in most," she said
soothingly. " A woman loves to have
secrets : it makes her feel so important.
I may have kept one from you." Then
she smiled at Northumberland.

" You are free to keep them all from
me, Madam," said Norris, resentfully.

" It would be wiser," she said angrily.

Defender of the Faith

"You are too hot-headed to govern your tongue. You'll ruin me yet. I have heard of your boasts."

"Who maligns me? — the musician?" cried Norris.

"Perhaps," she said, smiling. "I love him dearly. Poor little Mark! When I look at his forlorn tender face with those blue babyish eyes and that light fringe of his and listen to his piping and humble voice I am eager to put him in a cradle and rock him. I saw him this morning, and his smile was pathetic and welcome like a sunbeam in snow. Now, Mark Smeton is a considerate friend: he says it is enough for him to see me go by. I shall never be endangered by him. You know him, my lord?"

"I have heard him play for the Cardinal."

"You despise him? I'll tell you what

"The Queen of the May"

you overlooked in the letter. That miserable woman accused me of sending someone to poison her? Doctor Augustine, perhaps? Your eyes own it. Why should I care?" she went on, tossing her head. "Implacable hypocrite! The one thing she desired was revenge! You meant well; but you were wrong to suppress her accusation, believe me. Do you think anyone would attend to such folly?"

"I am glad to hear you say that," said Northumberland. "The King trusted me to read it all out. I can tell him about the sentence I skipped."

"Never! for God's sake!" she cried. "I mean — he is so stupid — men are always unjust."

"As you like."

"You stare as if you never saw me till now," she said, smiling.

119

Defender of the Faith

" I think I never did."

" Well, study me at your leisure, and then if a frail woman remains incomprehensible to her superior, a man — why, judge the best, my good lord. Ah! judge the best," she said, sighing. "That simple rule may be as conducive to justice as your masculine wisdom." Brightening, she went on, turning to Norris, " Will you defend me? Come, what am I like? "

" I 'll swear you are a good woman," said Norris.

" Well, you ought to know," she said, laughing. " But if I am so good why do you hesitate to go through with your wedding? Why should dainty Madge grieve? "

" I prefer to tarry," said he.

" Why? "

" Because I love one in your house better."

" The Queen of the May "

" Jealousy makes you bold," she said, laughing contemptuously. " You wish my lord to see you are favoured? You hang back from your marriage because you look for a dead man's shoes. The King has an incurable sickness. If anything should happen to him you would expect to have me? "

" If I had any such thought," replied Norris, " may my head be cut off! "

" Your head may be off then," she cried, " for I can destroy you. My lord's presence makes you courageous. I'll not be contented with a private servility. Never turn away! Contradict me now if you dare. You look for a dead man's shoes? "

There was a loud laugh behind her, and they all started back.

" A merry jest! " shouted the King, as he came out of the passage, shoving the

Defender of the Faith

tapestry aside with his shoulder. "What if the man had burnt his shoes before dying?" he said, pulling her ear.

The Queen tottered towards him.

"Harry, I had a right to overhear you in turn. Baby, you tremble," he went on, fondling her neck. "You are not frightened by your dull and sick husband? Ha! A good jest! I must share it with Cromwell, since you young people seem unable to relish it. There," he said, pushing her, "off with you! Run and play, children, and send Cromwell to me."

Then he sat down and lolled, laughing uproariously.

CHAPTER IV

As Northumberland followed the Queen
and Norris out of the room he saw Cromwell straddle at a window in the gallery,
appearing to watch the passers with a
curious benevolence. Cromwell turned,
scanning the Queen. Seeing Northum-
land, he lifted his eyebrows.

"The King desires your attendance,"
said Northumberland harshly.

"Eh? I thought he would," replied
Cromwell. "I delivered the key of a certain door to your wife. I had locked the
door for a little, not out of any ill-will to
you, but because I imagined you might
profit by hearing —"

"Where is she?"

Defender of the Faith

"I saw her go down the river. These variable, irrational women! She told me she had come in obedience to the royal command; but when I showed her in she drew back. Afterwards, when I gave her the key— One moment, my lord," he went on as the Earl was passing. "You have seen how things stand. Do you side with the Concubine or with her antagonist?"

"Sir," said Northumberland, "have the goodness to speak of her Majesty with befitting respect."

"Eh?" Cromwell said. "I am sorry."

The Queen and Norris had vanished. The Earl went down the wide stairs and so through the gardens to the bank of the Thames. Because only one boat was fastened there, and that had the royal arms on it, he was delayed for some minutes while another was fetched.

"The Queen of the May"

The weather had darkened. As he was rowed down the grey river his mind was still at the Palace. Passing the Temple, he was inclined to get out, as he had often done, and go up the narrow lane to the gate-house. It seemed to him he would find Aske busied with dusty parchments in his room there and they would chat with an affection they had never expressed. It seemed to him Aske would look up from his wide and short deeds, and discourse on the variance of writing as if nothing else was momentous.

As the boat left the Temple Garden behind he told himself their friendship was irrecoverable, and then his mind dwelt on Aske's house and he remembered its front decorated with the Cardinal's arms. That set him thinking how Sir Amyas Paulet had lived there and had placed those ornaments for a sign of repentance,

Defender of the Faith

because in his youth he had put a friendless wanderer in the Stocks and long afterwards met his forgotten victim as a Cardinal desiring revenge. Then he thought how his own life had proved bound by a shackle he had disregarded for years.

By Blackfriars he heard a voice summoning his boatmen to stop. For all answer they rowed harder, and one suggested they should make for the shore. "That is the King's boat," said the man.

Looking back, the Earl saw a boat coming with precipitate speed. "Stop," he said, turning.

As his rowers backed water he looked again at the other boat and saw Sir Richard Rich in the stern.

Slim and long Rich was wrapped in a big mantle of fur. As his boat came up he saluted Northumberland with an affable sweetness.

"The Queen of the May"

"My kind lord," he said gently, "I arrest you in the name of the King."

Drawing his sword, Northumberland took hold of its blade and proffered the hilt.

"I thank you humbly," said Rich, accepting the sword. "I shall not trouble you to step into my boat. I should be grateful if you would bid your men come with me."

Northumberland nodded to his men, and they pulled, and so the boats sped down stream till they stopped under the dusky arch of a gate. "Traitor's Gate," he said softly.

Paying his boatmen, he landed on the slippery steps. Rich got out also, and accompanied him up the steep path to the portcullis, and there asked for the Constable. Kingston came out, brisk and composed, followed by a peevish starved gaoler. His sharp black-bearded face

Defender of the Faith

was inscrutable, and he seemed to take the Earl's coming as a matter of course.

" Beauchamp — Banqueting-room," he said curtly.

Northumberland went with the gaoler, and was left in an airy and bright room on the first floor of the Beauchamp Tower by the Green.

The gaoler never took any notice of him. No offer of money could induce him to give tidings or take a message to anyone. The Earl spent much time at the window. So he saw the garrison drilled daily, and often watched lugubrious processions when the executioners dragged Catholics off to be hanged and quartered for denying the King's supremacy, or carried Lutherans away to be burnt. Frequently he heard music on the neighbouring river and guns fired on

the walls, and then knew the King was
passing to Greenwich. All day the mut-
ter of traffic surged round the ramparts.

So time went till one morning there was
a rejoicing of bells and the moan of traffic
was soft and was mingled with an echo
of carols. Because he had kept count of
the dates he knew the people were May-
ing. It was a bright morning, appropriate to May Day, and he fancied the
girls all in white hurrying to the woods
with their lovers to pluck hawthorn and
the flowers in the grass. Then he thought
of the times when he and the King and
Norris had worn golden masks and had
danced round the May-pole hand in hand
with the girls, heightening the popular
revels.

That morning silver trumpets were
clear on the Thames, and he pictured
Mistress Anne going by garlanded as the

Defender of the Faith

Queen of the May. Because the music was lasting he knew many courtiers accompanied her to share in her gladness. Then he thought of More's head spiked above her glittering triumph.

About noon a thunderstorm crashed. As the music did not return, he thought the King had decided to banquet at Greenwich on account of the tempest. The joy-bells were silent, and he heard only the reverberant thunder and the truculent rain.

Then there was a clashing of steel under the window. Looking out, he saw Norris, bareheaded and handcuffed and surrounded by guards, and in gilt armour as if he came from a tournament. Behind him little Smeton was struggling like a bird in a net. Then stamping feet mounted the stairs.

That afternoon the Earl watched with-

out seeing any one else. Next day he
stood at the window, and kept it open
because the weather was dark and sultry
as if thunder was near. The garrison was
under arms on the Green. Soon after
midday he heard tramping on the left, and
saw yeomen come, four abreast, and then
Kingston march, followed by the Queen
and a small cluster of ladies.

The Queen was in yellow, and wore a
round bonnet with a heavy white plume :
her dark hair hung dishevelled. Tears ran
down her cheeks, and she stooped as if
she was broken. As she passed the Earl
she looked up. Mopping her eyes hastily,
she struggled to look careless and proud.
Tossing her head, she turned to Kingston
and asked, " Is this to be my Palace
to-day ? "

Kingston told the yeomen to halt.

"No, Madam," said he. " His gracious

Defender of the Faith

Majesty has assigned you the rooms you had formerly."

" Before my coronation ? " she said. " It is too good for me — Oh, Jesus ! have mercy on me ! I thought prisoners were lodged in discomfort."

" Most of them are," he said.

"Poor souls ! " she sighed, and then with an air of childish curiosity asked, " Does anyone make the prisoners' beds ? "

" No, I warrant you," he said, taken aback.

" I wish I could do it for them. These little hands were not created for toil. Though I cannot make beds, I can make ballads. Well, now, there is none can do it better."

" Master Wyatt can," he replied.

" You said true. Wyatt loved me, as many have done, and like others he had cause to regret it. I remember he played at bowls with the King and they disputed a cast, for our gracious Lord will never own he is beaten. 'This is mine,' says Wyatt. 'Well, this is mine,' says the King, pointing, but looking down at his hand. Now he wore a ring he had wrested from me in sport, and he said this to triumph over Wyatt in turn. It has the King's portrait fastened under a ruby."

"Madam, we are delaying."

"Says Wyatt angrily, 'This is mine, then,' taking out an ivory tablet I had given him; and I assure you the boast came near removing his head. Yet in those days I had much power with the King. I had many a lover then — as you may remember — after my Lord of Northumberland's marriage."

"I must ask you to come with me, Madam."

Defender of the Faith

"What need of haste? I shrink from those walls. There I shall be friendless," she said, glancing at the ladies behind her. "I think it unkindness in the King to put such about me as I never loved. Lodge me in the Beauchamp Tower, Master Constable. Oh, Lord, help me, as I am guiltless! I hear say I shall be accused with two men, and I can do no more than deny it unless I open my body," she went on, clutching at the neck of her gown. "'Life would be bearable if hearts could be read,' says the King. Can I show him mine? Yet much would be bearable if I had a well-wisher near me. Let this be my Palace."

"No," said Kingston; "Sir Henry Norris is there."

With that she looked up at the higher windows, and then stretched out her arms. "Oh, Norris," she cried, "have you

"The Queen of the May"

accused me? You are in the Tower with me. You and I shall die together." Covering her face with her hands, she sobbed, "Oh, my mother! You will die of sorrow!" Then she looked up, saying, "Master Constable, shall I die without justice?"

"The King's poorest subject has justice," said he.

"I had forgotten it," she said with a laugh. "Sir, I shall detain you no longer."

Still laughing, she followed him across the Green to her prison.

That evening as Northumberland watched the dusk thicken till the opposite walls appeared shrouded in misty rain, he heard the lock creak.

"My lord," said Kingston as he stood on the threshold.

Defender of the Faith

"You come at last, sir?" said North-umberland. "You have shown me small courtesy."

"I am content to do my duty," said Kingston. "All prisoners are equal : it is my task to hold them in the name of the King. Ceremonious obser-vances—"

"Every man has a right to know the charges against him. Why was I—"

"That is no business of mine."

"I am glad you have come. Tell me what—"

"I am not employed as a purveyor of news."

"Then why am I honoured?"

"Because the King sends for you."

"At last."

"The guards are ready," said King-ston, going out of the room.

Taking his cap and cloak, Northum-

" The Queen of the May "

berland followed, and was led to the river.
The night was brooding and still.   There
was no moon, and the river was black,
but stabbed by wavy daggers of light
beside curtainless windows.   The hall and
the gallery of the Palace were thronged ;
but he went through the courtiers without
looking at any.   On the threshold of the
Red Room his guards handed him over
to the others there, and one of these
opened the big door and announced him.

The King was in purple, and sat in the
gilt chair while Cromwell stood on his right.
Playing at chess, they gazed down without
stirring.   Down the middle of the long
table lights in silver candlesticks gleamed
steadily though the windows were open.
Pausing by the threshold, Northumberland thought the players were breath-
less as if much was at stake.   Then the

Defender of the Faith

King put out his hand slowly and swayed it and shifted one of the ivory chessmen as if he feared the result.

" I take the Queen," Cromwell said, thrusting out his hand with a jerk.

The King dashed the inlaid board and the chessmen from the table and scowled.

Cromwell drew himself up and smiled, rubbing his hands. " Your Grace, here is my Lord of Northumberland," said he.

" Ha! back again, Harry? " said the King, lolling and drawing a breath as if he was rid of a weight. " Where have you been ? "

" In your Majesty's prison."

" It had slipped from my memory."

" May I ask what was my offence ? "

" Why did you lock him up ? " said the King, glancing at Cromwell.

" By your Majesty's orders," replied Cromwell obsequiously.

"The Queen of the May"

"Harry, it must have been on account of some trifling folly of yours. Boys will be boys. And these troubles — I had a foreboding of the issue of these affairs. I wrote a tragedy on it. Anne laughed at it — devil!"

"What affairs?" said Northumberland anxiously.

"Tell him about it," said the King lazily. "I am sick of it all."

"My good lord," said Cromwell as the King watched Northumberland, " our gracious master has met terrible grief. One he had raised from obscurity, a serpent nursed on his heart — "

"For God's sake, speak out," said Northumberland.

"I recoil from narrating such wickedness. In short, he has discovered Mistress Anne has been false to him."

"You lie," said Northumberland.

139

Defender of the Faith

"We are in the royal presence, my lord, but your heat is excusable."

"Or easily understood," the King muttered.

"Nothing would ever make me believe it," said the Earl.

"But she is prepared to confess —" Cromwell began.

"It is impossible."

"Further, her accomplices, Norris and Smeton, admit her guilt and their own."

"Norris!"

"Sir Henry Norris," said Cromwell. "And Smeton —"

"And is a lady to be dishonoured by the lies of —"

"A musician? Well, Norris is an unimpeachable gentleman."

"You knew nothing of all this?" said the King.

"The Queen of the May"

"I saw the Queen to-day," said Northumberland.

"Ha! you spoke to her?"

"No, I saw her led through the Tower."

"Go on," said the King, glancing at Cromwell.

"Our noble master is exempt from our frailty," said Cromwell, "and therefore blind to our sins. But his own eyes convinced him of her enormity yesterday. At Greenwich she was enthroned as Queen of the May, clad in yellow and wreathed in white roses, with her hair loose according to that immodest custom of hers. His gracious Majesty stood behind her while the nobles were tilting. As Norris passed her, she threw him a handkerchief. — Alas! that was a proof."

"That was only a favour," said Northumberland angrily.

Defender of the Faith

"It was a letter. The wretched woman had bribed Augustine to write on it with secret Italian ink, and he, shocked by her wickedness —"

"Betrayed her?"

"Enabled me to forewarn his Majesty; so her crime was detected. Then his Grace stopped the sports, and she was arrested with Norris as the thunder began."

"Ah, Harry," said the King with a sigh, "how my trusting heart was deceived! Yet I thank God for this unwelcome deliverance. The beauty of my soul has been marred by that indelicate girl! By nature I am profoundly religious; but she has led me in error."

"Power is granted to the Devil at times," said Cromwell sadly.

"If only my brother Arthur had lived! I would have been an excellent Pope.

" The Queen of the May "

Harry, she seduced me by witchcraft; so the marriage is void. You are a witness."

"Not I," said Northumberland scornfully.

"There," said the King, pointing over his shoulder solemnly, "you and I saw that vision in the Magical Mirror. Very true! The Devil has power. Thus she bleared my eyes once. A child of Satan she is — a pernicious Lutheran! Well, Samson was fooled, and even Solomon. Luther — that heretic! He called me a Thomistical ass!"

"Satan is a roaring lion," said Cromwell.

"Then I shall outroar him," said the King furiously.

"If anyone can," said Cromwell. "With the strength of Samson and the wisdom of Solomon — "

"And with my love of virtue," the

Defender of the Faith

King said. "My youth was apparently riotous; but I yearned to be holy. Harry, when I wake in the mornings I find my hands crossed on my breast: my mother taught me to fold them so when I was a child."

"Saintly in sleep!" said Cromwell.

"I wedded her because it was my duty to furnish England with Princes."

"God has not accepted the sacrifice, but has rewarded your Majesty by disentangling you from feminine snares."

"She was lovable once."

"But her beauty has gone."

"Very true," said the King. "Of late I have found her wearisome."

"A shallow and cruel —"

"She would give me no peace till I sent More to the block. Yet I had honoured him. How she hated the Lady Catherine also! Cruelty is unpardonable."

" The Queen of the May "

"Thoughtlessly cruel, eh?" said Cromwell as if he spoke to himself; "savouring her strength, like dear little children innocently torturing flies."

" I believed in her innocence long ago."

" Repose and innocence are imperfect unless they are unconscious," said Cromwell. " Mistress Anne was always playing a part. The world was her mirror. If she spoke alone with a man she imagined spectators : if she was with two her words to one were intended for the ears of the other."

"You speak as if she was dead," the King muttered.

"Your Grace," said Northumberland, " delusive confessions are easily extorted by craft. But even if she has sinned you will forgive her?"

" She has made me ridiculous."

Defender of the Faith

"Forgiveness is injustice," said Cromwell.

Said the King, "I may remind you of that."

"Before any tribunal, human or divine," replied Cromwell, "I would ask only for justice,—reward if I have earned it, and punishment if it is deserved."

"I shall remember."

"But she is so young," said Northumberland.

"And I am not," said the King. "Now I recall why I sent for you. There is a loophole.—If she was a Queen her crime would be Treason and punishable by death at the Stake. But if she was only—"

"The Concubine, as everyone called her," said Cromwell.

"I need not stoop to destroy her. I fear I am too mild. Still, I would prove

how little I am touched by her shame.
If I took vengeance ordinary fools would
believe I had been hurt by her; but if I
toss her to wallow in congenial disgrace
I can let the world see my gladness. It
was pleasant on the river last night after
the storm. We had music, and the ladies
were blithe. Then I read them my tragedy. Mistress Catherine Howard wept,
and said I was a prophet. A girl of fine
intellect — winsome and spirited! —
Harry, I'll read you the third act of it
when I am at leisure. Now, the other
was brainless — "

" God help her! she is a crowned
Queen," said Northumberland.

" But if my marriage with her was
void? "

" Induced by witchcraft? " said Northumberland, bitterly.

" Otherwise null," said the King,

frowning. "If she had been be-trothed —"

The Earl glanced at Cromwell.

"Ha! you understand?" said the King. "That is the loophole offering her a chance of escape. Are you aware of an original tie?"

Northumberland looked down.

"Where is that letter?" the King said, glancing at Cromwell. "Read it out," he went on, as Cromwell produced one from his belt.

"'This,'" Cromwell read, "'shall be to advertise you that Mistress Anne is changed from that she was when we three were last together. Wherefore I pray you do not suffer her in my absence to be married to any other man. Bid her remember her promise, which none can loose but God only.'"

"This is your writing?" the King asked, "she was betrothed to you?"

"The Queen of the May"

"In my presence," said Cromwell.

Said the King, "No dispensation was granted?"

"I have my lord's word for that," said Cromwell.

"Silent still?" said the King, "and yet a word will deliver her."

Said the Earl, "You have freed England from casuistical dotards."

"Must I treat you as a damnable heretic? It is my task to uphold the sacred laws of the Church. I am the Defender of the Faith. I studied Theology with care in my boyhood. Yet the Pope and the Cardinals controvert my opinion. So does Luther! Ignorant sot! He called me— Those miscreants are out of my reach. But you—"

"What should I say?" whispered Northumberland.

Defender of the Faith

"Merely the truth," said Cromwell.

"Have I your Majesty's word that my avowal would save her?"

"I have said it," answered the King. "I'll not stoop to revenge. She is too small to be punished. No! I'll not hurt the child."

"If unfaithfulness was the worst of her crimes," Cromwell put in.

"Then I admit she was betrothed to me once."

"Ha!" said the King. "This explains things I heard when you were last in this room. And that reminds me why I sent you to prison. I would have sent Norris with you; but Master Secretary persuaded me to leave him at large."

"For a time," said Cromwell.

"Till the proof was complete. Call the Constable of the Tower."

" The Queen of the May "

Opening the door, Northumberland saw Kingston and beckoned. Kingston came in, bending his knee.

" You have brought her ? " the King asked.

Kingston bowed.

" And Norris ? "

" Also," said Kingston.

" Is she — is she in tears ? "

" No, your Grace. She seems happy."

" Ha ! And this afternoon ? " said the King with a scowl.

" One hour she seemed determined to die, and the next much contrary to that," replied Kingston. " One minute she wept, and the next she was laughing. Sometimes she seemed to take much joy and pleasure in death. At other times she would offer to own anything if her life would be spared. Often her talk was wild."

Defender of the Faith

" Ha! What did she say ? "

" Foolish things. She asked whether anyone made the prisoners' beds, and said there would be no rain till she was out of the Tower, and we would see the greatest punishment that ever came to England if she should be murdered — "

" Who else is outside ? "

" The Duke of Norfolk."

" Bid him enter. Stay — where is Norris ? "

" At the end of the gallery."

" Good! You say she is not in tears ? Send her in."

CHAPTER V

THE King signed to Northumberland to come on his left. Leaning back as Norfolk entered, he stared at the table. Neither did he look up when an usher cried, " Room for the Queen."

The Queen came in, rosy and calm : her yellow dress was no longer disordered, and her dark hair hung smooth. Watching him mockingly, she stopped at the foot of the table, clasping her hands. Old Norfolk stood on her left : his stupid long face was still ; but he kept tugging his beard. Kingston stood on the threshold. All were turned to the King. After a time he glanced at Cromwell, and then looked down again.

Defender of the Faith

Said Cromwell, thrusting his hands under his belt, "You wrote begging our gracious master to see you."

"Alone," she said, smiling.

"That would be unseemly," said Cromwell; and she shrugged with a laugh. "In his great mercy he chose to confront you with your partners in crime."

Glancing round, she smiled at the King.

"Who are they?" she said. "Is my kind uncle of Norfolk one?"

Northumberland looked at her with a glimmer of hope. Cromwell nodded to Kingston. The Constable turned, and Norris came in handcuffed, with his eyes on the ground. Stopping on her right, he was motionless.

"One?" she said, smiling; but as she spoke she watched Norris and her bosom was heaving.

"There is another," said Cromwell.

Anna Bollein Queen.

"The Queen of the May"

The Queen glanced at Northumberland for the first time; and he met her eyes sadly. The hope that she would deny everything left him; and she only seemed brazen.

"Who?" said she.

"Master Smeton," said Cromwell.

"Where is he?"

"The man is sick."

"Tortured?"

"But he has signed a confession."

"On the rack?" she said scornfully. "The musician was never in my chamber but once, and that was at Winchester. I ordered him to play while I sang."

"He owns you inveigled him with money," said Cromwell.

"It is my custom to pay musicians," she answered. "I never spoke to him since, but on the Saturday before May-day, and then I saw him standing in the round window in my chamber of presence, and I asked why he was sad, and he answered and said it was no matter, and said I to him, 'You may not look to have me speak to you as I should to a nobleman, because you are an inferior person.' Said he, 'No, no, Madam, a look suffices, and thus farewell.'"

"The musician is a man of base blood, undeserving of a glance from a lady. You are accused by a gentleman of excellent birth."

"Is it true?" she said, turning to Norris, growing white and squeezing her hands.

"I accused you," said Norris, looking at her.

"Oh, Norris!" she whispered, shuddering and blinded by tears.

"And it was a lie!" he said, tossing his fetters.

" The Queen of the May "

" Ha! you dare?" cried the King, starting and scowling at him.

" A gentleman! yes! but disgraced. I was deceived into a lying confession. That villain," Norris said, looking at Cromwell, " promised to save her if I was a witness against her, swore she was doomed by Smeton's evidence and her sole chance of life lay in divorce, and I, tapped by my own folly, yielded. Jealousy led me to hint at favours I had never received. I could tear my tongue out — I am handcuffed — "

" Norris," the King said, " you were dear to me. Why should I blame you? Even I have been overcome by her witchcraft. You are a boy, a vain and hot-headed boaster. This shall all be forgotten. My painfully acquired wisdom was conquered — Lad, I forgive you. We shall be brothers again."

Defender of the Faith

"I can never pardon myself," replied Norris.

"A boy's passions!" the King said. "Elderly folk — "

"Forgive me, Madam," said Norris, kneeling.

She laid her hand on his head.

"Ha! you are obstinate to retract your confession?" said the King, clenching his fist.

Standing up, Norris said, "I had rather undergo a thousand deaths than betray the innocent. I have deserved them all. I lied in accusing her. Disgraced, I am a gentleman still."

"Hang him up, then," shouted the King, striking the table. "Hang him up!"

"My lord Duke," said Cromwell, as Norris went out, "this must be grievous to you. Do you think the evidence doubtful?"

"The Queen of the May"

The Queen looked at Norfolk with a despairing appeal.

"Alas, it is most plain," he answered, with his eyes on the King. "The abominable deeds done by my niece bring me into the greatest perplexity that ever poor wretch was in; for I fear that your Majesty, being so traitorously handled by one of my family, may conceive a displeasure in your heart against me."

As his thick voice stopped, she laughed.

"Master Cromwell," she said, "you told me my uncle of Norfolk has been long in your power —"

"Ha!" said the King, scowling at Norfolk.

"The Cardinal subdued him by holding proofs of his conspiring with Buckingham. Master Cromwell inherited —"

"Your Grace will not heed this shameless girl," Norfolk broke in.

Defender of the Faith

"For years, my loving uncle," she said, "I have helped Master Cromwell to keep you in disfavour, because I knew he could count on your assistance at need. I judged you well."

"Tut, tut, tut!" said old Norfolk, blinking at her. "Girl, though you never showed natural love —"

"I showed it too often, according to my enemies," she said, turning to Cromwell.

"You are not my enemy," he said, "but a criminal."

"And you the headsman?"

"If it was necessary. But our merciful Sovereign longs to give you time to repent."

Holding her breath, she looked at the King; but he still shunned her eyes.

"If you were the Queen and his wife —" Cromwell began.

"The Queen of the May"

"I am a crowned Queen of England and a true wedded wife."

"You are neither. You may have cause to be glad of it."

"You insult me with impunity though my husband and my subjects are here."

"Your alleged marriage was null."

"Because the Lady Catherine lived?"

"Because you had been already betrothed."

"Who are your witnesses?"

"I am one," replied Cromwell.

"Was your word ever believed?"

"There is the other."

"You have betrayed me, Harry?" she said. "Time tries all."

"Madam, it was for your sake," said Northumberland.

"You yielded, like Norris?"

"I owned the truth."

"And he? How do you know when

he was truthful? There are hours when a gentleman should lie for a lady." As she spoke she glanced at the King; but he did not seem to have heard. "I can still hurt *you*, Harry," she went on. "The old love is not dead. Ah! you are the origin of all my afflictions. If you had not deserted me —"

"You were the one to change," said Northumberland, under his breath.

"Oh, fool, to take a child at her word! We might have kept happiness if we could have seen one another with old eyes in our youth. We turned our backs on it — Whose was the fault? I sent you away; but how could I know your love was extinguishable by a petulant answer? Or is it shining still? Here, after that wonderful vision in the Magical Mirror, you were stern to me, claiming the immediate performance of my promise

to marry you. And I — well, I was
proud and not accustomed to harshness.
I have grown used to it since. I wept all
that night; but I was sure you would be
kind in the morning. A cold girl your
wife is — I remember her. You and she
are apart. I would have loved you in
degradation and shame." Then she
turned to the King : he still appeared
inattentive ; but his jaw drooped and he
seemed ailing and old. Sighing, she looked
at Cromwell, and then shrugged and went
on, " Have it all your own way. I have
given gold and costly presents to many.
I did it to overcome masculine virtue.
Repulsive to men, I had to bribe their
devotion. I have always been too lavish
with kindness. I remember letting my
Sovereign take a ring of mine once. Why,
he is wearing it now," she said, pointing ;
but the King did not stir. " I confess

everything. What infamy is a stain to a concubine? Let me go. I want to live out of England. I ask nothing else."

"Where do you wish to live?" replied Cromwell.

"Not in France — the people are glad, and I was happy in Paris: not in Italy — you have been there; — but in Flanders, for the Flemish are dull and unconcerned about strangers. I shall pass the time making ballads, merry ones now, for I am too sad to be doleful — songs with the summer in them. So shall girls yet unborn owe sweetness to things bitter to me. I shall make my brief greatness immortal by a ballad to be sung to the tune of 'Flying Fame.' My attendants shall be women, all old and beyond risk of corruption." Then she looked at Northumberland. "Parted only by distance, we shall be loving again, and shine to

" The Queen of the May "

each other like separated stars. Or will
you visit me when I am in Flanders?
You are free also. We may be happy
yet, as if we had never desecrated the
dreams of our youth — We were happy
once — do you remember? I was tempted
to show a King might be glad to have
the heart you abandoned. The King
mastered me: I used to be haunted by
his thunderous voice. I have often re-
gretted trusting to his passionate vows.
You should have seen how he grovelled
to me! I am too weak to be a mate for
a lion. A girl tires of a husband always
a King. Once he was a slave at my feet.
Now I am weary of hankering after ap-
proval like a bird hopping for customary
crumbs in the winter. I have learnt the
value of Fame — the moon's glint on the
hillocks of a tempestuous sea. Come
with me, Harry. Our path shines in

another country, and no remembrance
shall darken us when we have forded
Love's river of forgetfulness together at
last. I never loved the King," she went
on, after a pause. " No need to glance
at him : he is made deaf by an incurable
sickness. Besides, he is afraid of me.
To-night he has not looked at me
once."

The King looked up at her slowly.

"You can still hear ? " she said, laughing. Then she shrank, turning white.
"He said you would spare me," she
whispered.

Said Cromwell, "You would have
been spared if unfaithfulness had been
your only offence. But you have sur-
passed that iniquity. You sent Augustine to poison the Lady Catherine."

" *You* did."

"You have poisoned the King."

" The Queen of the May "

" God's wounds ! " cried the King, starting and glaring up at him sidelong.

" His Grace's royal body has suffered harm and danger through you. A minute ago you jeered at his illness. You were the cause of it."

" No, no," she said, laughing, "I am guiltless of that."

" You put an evil drug in his wine."

" When ? — " cried the King. " Where are my doctors ? "

" It was not deadly, though it has caused your Majesty's sickness," said Cromwell.

" Ha! you are sure it was not ? I have been a little feeble of late — "

Said Cromwell, " Bring Augustine in, Master Constable."

Clad in a gown of black velvet, the Venetian bustled in solemnly. Though he looked confident, his brown face was haggard, and his beady eyes wavered.

"Your Grace," the Queen said wildly, "I shall own everything."

"Good," said the King, watching her.

"I bought a love-philtre from Augustine: he swore it was harmless. I was desperate when I saw your love cease. Your sickness began long before that."

"Ha!" he said with a scowl.

"I know it is slight,—nothing," she stammered.

"Then I am neither deaf nor dying, you think?"

"I did not mean it. I was only trying to anger you — to make you speak to me."

"Be content," he replied.

"Catherine of Arragon was your enemy."

"So you said often."

"The Queen of the May"

"Her life was forfeit."

"And yours?"

"I besought you, time and again, to send her to the fate she deserved."

"Very true."

"Then one day last autumn I was walking in the garden at Hampton, miserable because you had been cold. It was a hazy afternoon, I remember, and a distant wind mourned, and the dead leaves wavered down like birds sinking irresolute when pastime is over. Thank God, it is summer now! — a lamenting wind would have maddened me. As I was moping, that knave," she went on, pointing to Cromwell, "came up to me, shambling like a ploughman whose feet are habituated to a burden of mud. 'Have you prevailed with his Grace yet?' said he. 'No,' said I. 'Eh?' he answered, 'he is afraid of the Emperor.'"

Defender of the Faith

"Ha!" said the King, glancing at Cromwell.

The Queen went on breathlessly, "'Yet,' said he, 'the Lady Catherine is but mortal, and her natural death would restore union with Spain. There may be found ways to rid England.' 'I have failed,' said I. Said he, 'It is my turn. I'll send Augustine to cure her. It is necessary. If the King feigns displeasure, I'll put the blame on Augustine — though I'll be reluctant, because he was kind to me when I was starving in Venice. Then he will be boiled in accordance with the King's jocular law.'"

"I will not," cried Augustine; but at a glance from the King he stopped, frozen by terror.

"'I'll have nothing to do with it,' said I," she went on, "'It is my turn,' he repeated. Never a word more did

" The Queen of the May "

I hear of it. I thought he had changed
his mind, and we quarrelled."

" Why ? " said the King.

" Because he made love to me."

The King laughed. "You make him
blush," said he, looking at Cromwell.

"Your Grace will not believe her,"
said Cromwell.

"A dainty lover ! " the King said.

She went on, "Said he, 'You and
I would be heads of an Evangelical
League. The King will soon be out of
the way. You shall be Regent while the
Princess Elizabeth —' Then I struck
him."

"Right ! " shouted the King.

" I swear it is false," stammered Cromwell.

"Till then," she said, "he had been
always behind me, urging me to be
merciless. Since, he has been in wait

to destroy me. The very morning
you heard of Catherine's death, I had
begged you to save England by judg-
ing her. Would I have done that if
I had known she was dying?"

"Women are full of tricks," said the
King.

"Your Grace has heard her desperate
lies," Cromwell broke in, "let me tell
the truth now."

"If you can."

"I have a witness," said Cromwell.
"Augustine will prove I had no hand
in it."

"Is that true?" said the King softly,
as he smiled at Augustine.

"I swear it is," he replied.

"And how," said the King with a
shudder — "how was it done?"

"I poisoned the wick of the lamp
kept burning at night by the Lady

"The Queen of the May"

Catherine's bed," answered Augustine, trembling, and looking at Cromwell.

"A poisoned lamp," muttered the King, "an allegory of Love. When was this?"

"Last October."

"A slow poison."

"But sure," said Augustine. "The Queen told me your Majesty ordered it."

"Ha!— and Master Secretary knew nothing about it?"

"Not a word."

"Did you furnish her with a venomous drug?"

"I did not know why she needed it, till your Majesty's illness made me suspect."

"And you wrote on the handkerchief?"

"What did I tell you to write?" she broke in.

Defender of the Faith

Said Augustine, " I dare not repeat it."

" Then I can," she said. " These were the words — ' Fly, you are in danger.' "

Said Cromwell, " Your Majesty has seen different words. They were only too plain when I had heated the handkerchief to make the ink legible."

" What reward shall be yours ? " said the King, smiling at Augustine with tenderness.

" I leave your Majesty to apportion it to my humble deserts."

" Good," said the King. " That is easy." Smiling still as his eyes dwindled he went on very slowly, " You shall be boiled."

" Misericordia ! " screamed Augustine, falling down on his knees.

The King waved his hand.

" I will not be boiled ! " shrieked Augustine, as the guards dragged him away.

" The Queen of the May "

The Queen trembled as she drew herself up.

"You have done justice," she cried. "Now send his accomplice to a merited doom."

" I shall," said the King.

"Look at him," she went on, pointing at Cromwell. "A picture of guilt! That sodden face of his is expressive at last."

"Your Majesty," stammered Cromwell.

" I look at the other poisoner now," said the King, watching her.

"You — you seek to frighten me!" she gasped, putting her hand up to her forehead.

"You admitted drugging my wine."

" A love-philtre, a charm," she cried.

"Your charms bewitch me no more. All my life has been poisoned by love," said the King, softly. " Is the mischief incurable? The Lady Catherine accused you. I overheard you thanking my dearest friend — your disdainful lover — for destroying her letter. I was fooled into prizing the heart his wisdom rejected. Shall I toss it aside for him to value again? Our mock marriage shall be undone by the Archbishop of Canterbury."

"I wish your Grace a worthier toy. I am one broken like that ivory queen," she said, pointing to the wreck of the chess. "I shall go to Flanders repentant. As I weep in my solitude I shall see you always further removed, as if we were sundered by a river that widens in perpetual rains. My shameful loveliness shall be hidden from all. There I shall be thrust aside like the Maypole of St. Andrew's, left desolate since Evil May-day. My palpitating heart will be quiet: your glory will leave it undis-

turbed, as the dawn triumphs without
rousing the dead. Is that thunder?"
she said, pausing and listening. "No, a
regiment passes. You fill London with
troops to make the people submissive?
I think England will pity me, for I have
done many good deeds. The morose
stuttering drums seem muffled as if they
throbbed at a burial."

"After the divorce," said the King,
"you shall be tried—"

"No!"

"Before the House of Lords."

"No—no! They are my enemies!"

"On the charge of being a poisoner."

"You kill me!" she sobbed. "Their
verdict is sure."

The King propped his head on his
hand and stared at the table.

"Because your guilt is undoubted,"
Cromwell put in, as if he thought the

Defender of the Faith

King wavered. "Surely they will condemn you to be burnt or hanged, as may please the King."

"Then I shall please him once again," she said, laughing. Clasping her hands, she cried feebly, "For God's sake, hear me — my King! my husband! — I love you alone!"

"To-night," said Cromwell hurriedly, "while you jeered at his Majesty's sickness you insulted him by owning your love for a young — "

"Oh, my King!" she sobbed, "I was frenzied by your sullen contempt. I did not know what I said — "

"The truth comes out in anger," the King muttered.

"My heart is yours only."

"Then I fling it away."

"See, I speak honestly — I did not love you at first."

"The Queen of the May"

"Ha!" he said, looking up.

"I married you to be Queen. I despised you for letting me subdue you so easily —"

"What?" he cried.

"How can a girl know her own heart? Mine wavered and was never at rest. Now I am a woman. This night has added a score of years to my age. And I worship you."

"Too late," he said.

"My love is born of terror," she cried. "You are a King."

"A girl tires of a husband always a King," he muttered.

"But a woman does not. When I said that —" Then she burst into tears.

Looking at Kingston, he said, "Let her be taken back to the Tower."

Shutting his eyes, he leant back. As Kingston came she drew herself up.

Defender of the Faith

"My weakness is past," she said.
"Never again shall I vex you with irrepressible tears. When hope is gone, courage revives. I am a daughter of the Howards and worthy of my illustrious uncle. If it would please you as much, I had rather be beheaded than hanged or burnt, for I have played at being a monarch. Mine was the short triumph of a Queen of the May. I hear say the executioner is very good; and I have a little neck," she went on, laughing and clasping her hands round it,—"a tiny neck, Cophetua. Look up! I am not crying. Shall I cheer you by singing? What song shall I choose?—the rhyme I made while we watched your troops going past as they do yonder?"

Then she began singing recklessly, in a quavering voice:

"The Queen of the May"

"King of the weary land, enthroned on high !
We, slaves of your command, go out to die.
Indifferent above, you trifle thus ;
The simple things we love are lost to us."

"Not always indifferent," muttered the King.

"My simple joys," she said, laughing. "I played with love. I am punished. I was eager to love all who seemed friendly. Now I am friendless."

"No," cried Northumberland. Springing forward, he clasped her hand, kneeling.

Snatching her hand back, she said, "Keep your kisses for the Lady Magdalen, if she will accept them. Be loyal to her, though you were faithless to me. No man shall touch me again till the executioner does."

"I forgot you, Harry," said the King, looking up as Northumberland rose.

Defender of the Faith

" The dead man's shoes were to have been
your inheritance?   Ha! When the Pope
sent the Bishop of Rochester a Cardinal's
hat, I said 'Good! when it arrives the
Bishop can wear it on the stump of his
neck.'   A merry jest and prophetic!   My
shoes pinched me, dear brother: I'll put
you out of reach of such pain.   Take him
back to the Tower, Master Constable."

" I go gladly," said Northumberland.
" God knows I am weary of life."

" Why should you hurt him when the
worn shoe is destroyed?" she said as she
looked at the King.

" To double assurance," he replied, gazing down.

" Poor Harry," she said as she took
Northumberland's hand, " we must make
friends.   Shall we go on the river again
to-night as we used?   It is dark on the
water, and the tide is at full."

"The Queen of the May"

"Anne, forgive me!" he whispered.

"I spoke in bitterness, Harry. I did not mean it."

Holding his hand, she turned and smiled at the King.

"I thank you for all your favours," she said. "You changed the cowslip crown into gold. Discontented with that, you are giving me the crown of a martyr, royal Cophetua. You can do nothing more for me; but I beg you to cherish our little daughter Elizabeth. Pining for a son, I was cold to her. Elizabeth will never remember motherly love. If I am judged to death according to law I shall say nothing against it. Your poorest subject has justice. I shall accuse none; but I shall pray God save you and send you long to reign over England. A more gentle or mild Prince never swayed sceptre. Your bounty and clemency towards

Defender of the Faith

me, I am sure, have been especial. If anyone intends an inquisitive survey of my
actions I require him to judge the
best. Come with me, Harry," she
went on, turning away, "the King has
united us."

"Take them apart," the King muttered, without lifting his head.

"Love perishes; but jealousy thrives,"
she said.

On the threshold she paused and
looked at the King as if she hoped at
the last. Then she turned, shrugging
and laughing. The King groaned and
stopped his ears.

BOOK III

Pilgrims of Grace

CHAPTER I

As the door was shut by a guard the Queen broke down and cried bitterly with her face in her hands. While she stumbled along the gallery, Northumberland followed her, but was checked at the top of the stairs for some minutes, and then led to the river and taken back to the Tower. There he was put in a Beauchamp cell lit by a barred hole in the roof.

So he fretted without news of the world till a dark evening in autumn. Then while a fog seemed to make his prison remote from London he heard

Defender of the Faith

a clatter of keys, and Rich came in, wrapped in his luxurious mantle.

"I come from my Lord Cromwell," said Rich as he bowed.

"Then go back," said the Earl without rising. "I have no dealings with him."

"You are unjust to him, my dear lord."

"I guess your errand," said Northumberland scornfully. "You were sent here to trap Sir Thomas More by feigned sympathy. When he was judged you accused him of denying the King's supremacy of the Church at that meeting. More called you a liar; but your evidence doomed him. Imagine I have said all you want."

"You are ungenerous to me, too," said Rich. "I bring freedom."

"On what terms?" said Northumberland, rising.

Pilgrims of Grace

"You are to go back to Wharfe."

"Where is Lady Northumberland?"

"There."

"Where is the King?"

"At Windsor; but it is said he will ride to crush the rebels of Lincoln."

"Is Lincoln in arms?"

"The clergy and the ignorant rustics and a half-hearted throng of the gentlemen are briefly allied against their different grievances. Sixty thousand are in arms in the Fens."

"And Yorkshire?"

"Is quiet," said Rich, "but the King has need of friends in the North."

"So repents keeping them imprisoned unjustly?"

"My Lord Privy Seal — perhaps you are unaware my Lord Cromwell has been advanced to that post? — has chosen this time for proving his belief in your loyalty. I wish I could persuade you he is truly your friend. And his kindness is valuable. See how he protected Augustine —"

"That villain was spared?"

"He escaped from the Tower. I suspect my Lord Privy Seal delivered him and keeps him in hiding; for he is the kindest of men, though we may consider him unscrupulous in matters of State. Because he looks on such things as a student, he is not hampered by tenderness. You or I might have spared Mistress Anne."

"Was she killed?" said Northumberland.

"The poor soul was beheaded out there on the nineteenth of May. I was on the scaffold with my Lord Cromwell and saw her die merrily. With her last breath she praised the King's justice and peculiar clemency. The next morning he wedded Mistress Jane Seymour."

"God forgive him!"

"Some hoped he would have married Mistress Catherine Howard. You know her, my lord?"

"Yes."

"A dear friend of mine."

"When can I go?"

"As soon as you like," said Rich, bowing. "Your people at Northumberland House have been forewarned of your coming, and your sword has been sent there. One of your men — your foster-brother, I think — is waiting outside. With your permission, my kind lord, I shall leave you."

Bowing low, he withdrew.

Then Allan Thorne came in stolidly. The sight of that sunburnt round face of

Defender of the Faith

his with the colourless eyebrows and the steady blue eyes made the Earl think of lost happiness. Walking to Northumberland House, he armed and took horse and then rode Northward with Thorne.

Reaching Lincoln, he found the Cathedral garrisoned for the King, while the troops huddled beneath it. The citizens looked dark and morose, and kept away from the soldiers. From an innkeeper he learnt how the rebels had quarrelled and had abandoned the city that morning at daybreak and had gone to their homes.

Sending Thorne to prepare Lady Northumberland, he travelled with a slackening speed. The moors were silvered by rain, and a wind stole by with little footsteps. It was a black midnight when he mounted the hill sheer beside Dead Man's Ford. Nearing the top, he saw a pile in front of him like a small haystack, and then a horseman beside it, blocking the narrow path. Then he heard Aske's voice, "Who goes there?"

"Answer, if you are a friend," said Aske, after a pause. "No stranger passes to-night."

"We were not always strangers," said Northumberland softly.

"Harry!" cried Aske. Then he said, "You here, my Lord of Northumberland?"

"Let me by."

"As a friend?"

"You broke our friendship."

"As a rebel?"

"As the King's loyal servant."

"Return then to Cromwell and your chosen allies."

"I mean to pass," said Northumberland, drawing his sword.

"And I am here to prevent it."

"My sword is out."

Defender of the Faith

" And mine."

The Earl charged, and the blades clashed sparkling, and he felt a blow on his side, as Aske's horse went down. Springing from his saddle, he stood on guard. " Are you hurt, Rob ? " said he, as the horse floundered up.

Sheathing his sword, he took out his flint, and struck it, and saw Aske lying prone. " If only I had a light ! " he said. Groping, he felt the heap on his left and found it was brushwood. Then he knelt and set the brushwood on fire. As the pile crackled under clambering flames, Aske got up, staggering, with his hand on his forehead.

" Are you wounded ? " said the Earl.

" I was stunned by the fall," said Aske, as if he was dazed. Then he stared at the light. " Who lit it ? " he went on.

" I did, to see how you were hurt."

Pilgrims of Grace

An alarm bell began to clash in the valley, and was answered by others on the northern moors. The Earl saw a fire aloft in the distance. Then he watched others leap as if the hills spouted flame.

"God's ways are unfathomable," said Aske. "You have summoned the Catholics to rise, after all."

Folding his arms, Northumberland looked at Aske without speaking.

"Harry," said Aske, "God has recalled you. You have been driven out of His path by irresistible trouble. Mistress Anne is gone now. May she rest in peace! Nothing need part you from your wife. I was waiting for a message from Lincoln. If the news had been favourable I would have lit the beacon at four. I am only a follower of the Catholic lords. You are our loved leader again."

Defender of the Faith

Northumberland gazed at the beacons: they seemed to him torches uplifted by invisible giants. Rough villages in the clefts of the moors and old solitary castles and fishers' huts by the sea and monasteries hidden in woods were being thrilled by that shining. In numerous homes it was the signal for parting. Women were crying as they buckled on the men's armour. Thousands were risking everything for a desperate hope. Then he pictured his wife watching the beacons with their child in her arms at the window of the parlour at Wharfe. Was she thinking how they would have called to him in the time when she loved him? Was the Friar with her? he wondered. Then he thought of the Cardinal, and remembered the grasp of his soft and feverish hand as the old man saw a vision.

Pilgrims of Grace

"It is too late," he said, echoing the Cardinal's words.

Sighing heavily, Aske stooped for his sword. Northumberland reeled, suddenly dizzy, and then clapped his left hand to his side, remembering the blow he had felt. Finding his hand wet, he looked at it and saw it was bloody. Wiping it on the inside of his cloak as Aske rose, he said faintly, "Will you let me pass now?"

"You go to Wharfe? I'll accompany you. I wish to see Friar Anderton."

So they led their horses down the steep path. Mounting, they splashed through Dead Man's Ford while a flush scurried on the tremulous river. Then they rode up the naked moor on the left. On its crest a huge beacon towered as if it was scorching the sky. As the roar of that great bonfire grew faint behind them, they heard a psalm.

Defender of the Faith

Going round the edge of the moor, they met a procession. First came armed horsemen with torches and banners, and then an old priest in gilt vestments rode carrying a tall silver cross, and behind him were many monks, riding two abreast, with swords dangling beside their rosaries, followed by other troopers and by archers on foot.

Northumberland screened his face with his cloak, and drew rein by the roadside. Aske copied him, as the procession approached chanting " Exsurget Deus."

Seeing them, the first horseman paused, and then the others stopped also.

" Friends or foes ? " said the horseman.

" Who are you ? " replied Aske.

Pilgrims of Grace," was the answer.

" Who is your leader ? "

" Robert Aske."

Pilgrims of Grace

Startled, Aske let his cloak fall, and so the man recognised him. "The Captain!" he cried, and his shout was repeated down the array.

"My son," said the old priest, riding forward, "we have come at your bidding. Take this. You are the one to lift the Cardinal's cross."

"My bidding?" said Aske.

"Your proclamation has been posted to-night on the market-cross and the church. Your messengers are scouring the hills."

"Mine?" said Aske, as if he was wondering. Then he lifted his voice. "Go forward in God's name. I shall be with you to-morrow."

With a renewed acclaim the procession wound beside the edge of the moor. So Aske and Northumberland went into the village of High-thorpe, screening

Defender of the Faith

their faces. There they found the women and children and feeble elders agog as if it was market-day. The first they met was an old shepherd, tottering as he leant on his crook, laughing extremely. " There is a madman in the cage on the Green," he cried, " and his language is hideous."

As Aske paused by the market-cross, stooping to read a notice stuck on its shaft, Northumberland looked over the bystanders and saw a man in the cage. The prisoner was muffling his face in his hood, and cowered back in the corner. There was something familiar in his dangerous crouch.

" The hand of God again," said Aske slowly. " I never issued that summons. Yet there it calls the country to rise, and it is signed with my name."

" Find out who the prisoner is," said the Earl.

Pilgrims of Grace

"What has he done?" said Aske to a young woman beside him.

"We caught him prowling to-night," she said, tittering. "Some were going to hang him as a spy; and then he was so savage that we saw he was mad."

"Who are you, knave?" said Aske as he looked down at the prisoner.

"One you know well," the man muttered as if he spoke through clenched teeth.

The Earl turned away and let his cloak fall.

"Hold my name secret if you value your life, Master Aske," the man said, springing forward.

"The Captain," cried some of the bystanders. "A Percy! a Percy! my Lord of Northumberland and the Captain are with us! God save our noble leaders!"

"Stand back, good people," said Aske,

dropping his cloak. The crowd drew aloof and gaped at them reverently.

"I set small value on your chance of life, my Lord Cromwell," he went on softly as he stooped to the cage.

"I am in your hands," replied Cromwell. "You will find it worth your while to assist me."

"I would be the last to lift a finger to help you," said Aske. "I have but to name you and your shrift will be short."

"Then, my Lord of Northumberland, I appeal to your loyalty."

"What brings you here?" said Aske slowly.

"I was bound for Wharfe," answered Cromwell. "I left my men, and came here to see for myself how the villagers were receiving the summons. I was surprised by the muster."

Pilgrims of Grace

" I 'll not shed your blood," said Aske
scornfully.

" Then you 'll free me ? "

" By no means."

" If you leave me here, some of the
gathering rebels will recognise me to-
morrow."

" So I hope."

" I 'll spare him," said Northumberland, turning.

" Why ? " said Aske.

" Because he is my enemy."

" Do as you think best."

Then the Earl ordered the rustics to
set the prisoner free, and rode on.

When he came to the Wharfe with
Aske in the small hours of the night he
thought the voice of the river was full of
frenzied despair. There was a dull pain
in his side, and he felt his clothes stick-

Defender of the Faith

ing clotted. In his heart there was a similar ache. Unmanned by weakness, he felt as if he was small again, riding home on his pony, wondering at the rage of the Wharfe and the misery of the wind in the trees. Now the woods were unstirred; but a far clamour of bells haunted him like a storm overhead.

Going round to the front of the Castle, he saw torches flock up the long avenue. The wide door was ajar, and the steps and gravel were shining. The clattering hoofs summoned his men. Getting out of the saddle, he almost fell, and he found it hard to go up the steps. As he crossed the threshold the Friar welcomed him and said the child was asleep. " Poor darling ! " he said, " she could not keep her eyes open. I was afraid she would take cold."

" It is good to be home," said Northumberland faintly.

Pilgrims of Grace

With that he looked at the stairs ; but he was afraid to go up them for fear his plight should be evident. So he turned to the left and went into the dining-hall. Sinking into the high chair at the head of the table, he whispered, " Bring me some wine ! "

Dizzy and swooning, he leant back, shutting his eyes. When he opened them, he saw a goblet, and took it with an irresolute grasp. As he drained it there was shouting outside, " A Percy ! a Percy ! God save the Earl of Northumberland."

Then he looked to the right, and saw Aske stand by the window, and heard cheers for the Captain. Staring in front of him, he watched the high doorway. It seemed to him his wife must come lovingly. The trouble that sundered them was far from his mind. Then his

Defender of the Faith

heart rose and there were tears in his eyes ;
for she came just as he hoped. Clad
in grey riding-clothes, she stood on the
threshold, and held a big banner in her left
hand while her other was stretched to him.

" Now welcome home," she said, " and
never so welcome."

The words chimed in his heart as the
bells had done at his wedding. Checked
by his stillness, she winced as if she
was frightened. Then she came forward
slowly with a confident pride.

" My lord," she said softly as she
paused on his left, " here is your banner."

Looking away from her eyes reluctantly, he glanced at it, and instead of the
White Lion saw a cross and such emblems
as he had seen on the standards of a
religious procession. " Where ? " he asked
himself. Then he recalled seeing such a
banner that night.

Pilgrims of Grace

"It is not mine," he said faintly.

"It is the banner of the Five Wounds," she said, "the standard of the Pilgrims of Grace. It is all my work, dear. See, I am wearing the badge of the Five Wounds, for I shall go at your side. Lady Bulmer and other women intend to share the lot of their husbands; so I shall have feminine company while you are in battles. I have burnished your armour and set it out in your room. We shall never more be parted again. I knew God would answer my prayers. Blessed be His name for ever!"

Still he looked up at her while his sick heart thirsted for the love in her eyes.

"You are so pale, my husband. I have been ill also; but you have cured me to-night," she went on. "Hear how your people worship you! All over the North the runners hasten to tell how you

joined the Pilgrims at High-thorpe. I
cried for gladness when they brought me
the news; but I would not meet you with
tears. Why are you silent?" she whispered, shrinking away.

"It is not true," he said hoarsely.

As his eyes grew dim he thought she
was far. Outside the cheering redoubled,
"Esperance Percy! The Earl shall be
our King!"

Bowing her head, she clutched the back
of his chair.

"It may yet be true," said Aske, coming forward.

Starting, she looked up at him, saying,
"I did not see you."

Then in ran the Friar, carrying little
Cecily reverently. "I have brought her,"
he cried. "Poor baby! She is still half
asleep."

Pilgrims of Grace

Northumberland did not move to receive her. Cecily cringed as if she was alarmed by a stranger. The Friar looked from one to another as if he was dismayed but taking a puzzled delight in this incomprehensible world.

"And you?" said Lady Northumberland to Aske. "Are you the Captain, or is that also a lie?"

"For lack of a better leader," he said, "I am the Captain."

"Then I have one to trust," she said, and proffered the banner.

Aske leant across the table and took it.

"It is not mine yet," he said. "Harry! for the last time I appeal to you."

"My mind is made up," said Northumberland as if he spoke in his sleep.

"Yet think again," said Aske. "Since Mistress Anne is dead now, your marriage to her ladyship can be repeated, and —"

Defender of the Faith

"What do you mean?" she whispered.

"Though my lord was betrothed to Mistress Anne—" said Aske.

"Betrothed to that vile woman—marriage repeated—" she said faintly. "You mean—my marriage was—this is madness!" Turning, she clasped the child to her heart. "Speak!" she said feverishly to Northumberland. "You sit like a stone. Tell him—tell him he raves." Gazing at him, she drew herself up, and then thrust the child back to the Friar; but as he was taking it she hugged it again. Kissing it, she looked up at Aske slowly. "And you knew this?" she said.

"Since before the Cardinal died."

"The one I trusted!"

Turning, she gave the child to the Friar.

"Did you?" she said as he took it.

"God forgive me! I did," said he.

"All this long time!" she said.

"I could not bring myself to tell you. You and my lord were living apart. I put it off."

There was a throbbing of drums and then the shout of a trumpet.

"A Darcy!" the mob roared by the window.

Then in strode Lord Darcy, armed from head to foot, wearing the badge of the Five Wounds on his breast.

"Harry, I wronged you!" he cried, holding out his arms as he came. "My friend's son — my own boy!"

Then he stopped and looked at the Countess. Behind him the rebels rushed in, shouting, "Esperance Percy!"

Northumberland sprang up, crying, "Back! This house shall not be dishonoured by rebels."

Defender of the Faith

There was a minute's silence, then shouting "Down with the Traitor Earl! Strike off his head!"

As old Darcy drew his sword frantically and the rebels surged forward Northumberland reeled.

"I can die but once," he said. "It will rid me of my pain. I am alone against the world. God knows I wish myself out of it!"

"I am with you, my lord," said Allan Thorne, striding forward.

Northumberland staggered and held out his arms with bitter tears in his eyes.

"My brother," he whispered, and fell prone on the rushes.

"Oh! poor child!" sobbed his wife, kneeling beside him.

As she lifted his head, cherishing it, he opened his eyes and gazed at her with incredulous happiness. Rising, she let him go, and he sank fainting again. As Thorne stooped the Friar said, " He is wounded ! My lady, there is blood on your gown ! "

As she looked at the stain Aske cried, " Wounded ! I must have done it ! "

" You ? " she said, shrinking.

Thorne glared at him as if he would have flung himself on him, and carrying the Earl, broke through the crowd.

Northumberland came to himself lying on the bed in his room. At first he did not know where he was. Remembrance came back like the miserable dream of a fever. A man stood by his side: it was himself, he thought — how could this be? That was his black armour, there was the White Lion embroidered over the breast-plate. The man's face was hidden, for the vizor was down.

" What—who are you ? " said the Earl softly with a tremble of awe.

Defender of the Faith

"Your loving servant," answered Thorne's voice.

"Those are my arms."

"The rebels went out," said Thorne, "but they are raging beneath, threatening to kill you when their leaders depart."

"Let them do it."

"Not while I live. I shall confront them. They will take me for you. This is your armour; but I wear my own sword. I have one blow to strike. Then I shall break them. It is the only hope."

"I forbid it," said Northumberland, attempting to rise.

"For the first time I disobey you, my lord."

As Thorne went the Earl struggled to rise, feeling chained. Staggering to the window and pulling it ajar, he leant out. "I — I am Northumberland!" he cried; but his voice whispered unheard.

Pilgrims of Grace

Aske was on his horse by the door, lifting the banner of the Five Wounds, while Darcy was in the saddle beyond him. Behind them a multitude swarmed with banners and torches. A grey riderless horse was held at the other side of the door. Lady Northumberland was on the steps, holding the child. The Friar stood at her back. As Darcy and Aske bowed to her there were cries in the mob, " The Earl comes ! A Percy ! "

Then Northumberland saw his foster-brother on the top of the steps. Again that shiver came over him as if he looked at himself. Lady Northumberland turned to Thorne, crying, " My husband ! " Thorne drew his sword and sprang down and lifting it high, struck at Aske ; but his blow was impeded by the staff of the banner. Aske reeled away, clutching the end of the cut staff

Defender of the Faith

while the banner was falling. The rebels rushed, and Thorne charged them, hacking to right and left, and reached the planks on the Wharfe. Then he staggered and flung up his hands and fell headlong into the river. The rebels pursuing him stopped. One cried, "The Traitor Earl drowns!"

Northumberland looked back at his wife and saw her stand like a statue and then thrust the child into Friar Anderton's arms. Picking up the banner, she mounted and rode away beside Aske.

CHAPTER II

NORTHUMBERLAND stood clutching the
window and then crossed the room
blindly and reeled down the dark stairs.
The hall was forsaken. Going out by
the postern, he staggered through the
trees till he halted where the Wharfe
shouted in the pit of the rocks. Hidden
in the black gulf at his feet, it rushed
clamouring as if it exulted. A hope of
saving his foster-brother died as he listened: no man could escape from that
tumultuous river.

Torches were jumping in the night of
the wood, and he fled from them, trip-
ping over briars and stones. The torrent
dismayed him as if he writhed in its grip;

Defender of the Faith

but it mastered him, and he kept on its brim. No cry for help mingled with its passionate voice. Coming at last to a narrow bridge, he went on it and leaning on ivy, stared down, taking breath. White flashes sprang underneath : one was the plume of a helmet, he thought, and another a glimpse of his armorial Lion. Then he knew they were foam. The wild river called to him, offering him sleep after pain ; but he broke from its spell and made for the North. When that grim chant of the Wharfe waned his heart rose. The Earl of Northumberland was gone in the dark. No more a lord, but a nameless man out of the fetters of life, he was alone.

From time to time he looked back, instinctively afraid of pursuit. Often a breeze wafted a far discord of bells ; but they concerned him no longer. Night

Pilgrims of Grace

made the country peaceful till dawn came
back with banners. Topping a black
eastern hill, they were distinct against the
glimmer of morning. Now he was indifferent to their tidings of battle.

It seemed to him he wandered many
miles, with clogged feet and dim eyes and
a resting heart, before the strength of his
fever gave out and he sank upon a pillow
of moss. When he came to himself his
head was on a billet of wood and he was
lying on a mat made of rushes. Looking
up, he saw rafters with smoke drifting
about them like incense in the roof of a
church. Gazing round stupidly, he saw
he was in a bare little hut. On his left a
shaggy brown dog crouched, watching
him soberly. On his right a pot hissed
on a fire. Another bed with a shepherd's crook and some wooden platters

Defender of the Faith

and mugs thrown on it completed the furniture.

Sitting up and rubbing his eyes, he found he was bearded. As the dog leapt up, wagging its tail, and ran out of the hovel, he went to the threshold. The first thing he saw was a rabbit seated demurely, washing its mild face in the rain. Then he saw uplands ghostly in a quivering shower. On those autumnal moors silence was absolute.

So he stood drinking the lofty air for a time. Then he heard barks and a piped ballad approaching. Somebody shrilled "The Hunting of the Cheviot" in the mists on the right.

> "The Percy out of Northumberland,
>   And a vow to God made he
>   That he would hunt in the mountains."

Thus the voice whined, and then a tattered old shepherd came slowly, with

the dog at his heels. This was a feeble
scarecrow with a face like a goat's; and
he was shining with happiness. Seeing
Northumberland, he grinned and nodded,
and hurrying his difficult steps, lifted his
voice, —

> " ' They were twenty hundred spearmen good,
> Withouten any fail :
> They were born along by the water of Tweed
> In the bounds of Teviotdale.'

" A merry world !" he said. " So you
have found reason at last? The things
you have been saying ! — oh, good lord !
I did laugh."

" How did I come here?" said Northumberland, flushing.

" On my cart. The Bishop found you
with your nose in the moss ; and I near
broke my spine in lifting you up."

" What Bishop ? "

" Dear, dear," said the shepherd, " I

thought the whole country knew my dog
was named Bishop because he has to look
after a flock. It is but one of my jests.
No doubt you are a stranger. Good dog!
Watch him trying to laugh. I had been
down to High-thorpe."

"Ah!" said Northumberland, remembering where he had seen the shepherd
before.

"You wonder?" the old fellow went
on. "Yes, I am a traveller. Twice
every year I go away to the market. The
things I have seen! That very night
there was a lunatical knave — good lord!
my ribs were sore with my mirth. What
a night that was! Never did I encounter
so many marvels, and yet I have gone
travelling — as every one knows — twice
every year. That night I saw the Traitor
Earl with these eyes."

"Indeed?"

Pilgrims of Grace

"Not that I saw his face — no! thank Heaven! for they say it was frightful, as was but natural since he was possessed by the Devil. I happen to know that as a fact. There he was riding with his cloak held up thus and his eyes glowering above it like embers. The Devil was staring out of his head. To think of it! I used to be so eager to look at him: he owned all these moors away for hundreds of miles. Till then I had missed him: it used to make me so wild I could have eaten my hands. Yet I saw him before the Devil carried him off."

"Did you see that too?"

"I heard of it from black William, a pedlar, yet a trustworthy man. Surely you know him? Where do you live? Says William, meeting me as I was coming along before the Bishop found you, — says he, 'Satan has the Traitor Earl —

Defender of the Faith

swooped on him as he was crossing the bridge by the Castle — I saw it.' 'Thanks be to God,' says I. 'So say all of us,' replies he. 'Tell me more,' I shouted; but he was gone. Black William is a man of his word. So am I. True Barnabas Sykes, they call me : you must have heard of me often. Old Barnabas, some call me of late. I 'll scrape the moss from their tombstones yet when I go marketing twice every year."

"Then I have to thank you for saving me."

"Could I leave you to die alone on the moor ? I nearly did when I found you were as heavy as lead. I am not as strong as I was, but I am good for many a winter."

"To repay your kindness —"

"The wound was ugly, and your fever was horrible. You repaid me at once, for you were enlivening company. 'Gentle Magdalen,' says you, 'beautiful Magdalen.' How I did laugh! 'Sweetheart,' says you, kissing my hand — this very hand," said the shepherd, looking at his stained fingers. "No one ever kissed it before. 'Rob will make you happy,' says you; 'you should have married him. Now I am dead, you will forget me, love, and all will be well. Delicate Magdalen,' says you, 'oh sweet Magdalen.' Then you would turn over, and cry, 'It is too late. Merciful God! It is too late.' Then you would begin calling me Anne. 'Be true to me, dear: and then no one shall come between us,' says you, 'not the proud Cardinal — no, nor the King. God save the King!' you would shout, waking the Bishop. Lord, how he barked, the time you wanted to murder me! 'It is all your work, miscreant,' you cried, grip-

Defender of the Faith

ping my throat. 'Rob is my friend,' says you, 'a noble gentleman. The King is my brother. — Let me hold your yielding chill little hand once again, for the last time, for a minute, my wife, Magdalen.'"

"No more of that," said Northumberland.

"As you like it, your Highness."

"Why do you address me so?"

"The King's brother is a prince," said the shepherd. "You know I must have my jest. Merry Barnabas, the girls used to call me. Old Barnabas, that little fool said — she does not know any better."

"I have but little gold."

"I know you have a fortune. Seven gold pieces! When did I see so many? I put them under your mat."

"If you will accept them —"

"Lie down and rest. I hoped the fever was gone."

Pilgrims of Grace

"I think it is. They are yours, and I shall trespass no longer —"

"You are unforgiving," the shepherd said peevishly. "I did not mean to offend."

"On the contrary, I am most grateful."

"Come in, then. The Bishop is hungry. Hark how the pot sings on the fire."

So a long association began. With rough food and the incurious society of sheep and the blithe prattle of their owner, the days were swift to Northumberland. Dawn summoned him to foster the sheep. It was a dangerous task often, for the winter was hard, and the drifts blocked the hut, choking the wattled folds. Spring brought the need of midwifery for the ewes in their trouble. When his clothes were worn out he borrowed a ragged smock from the shepherd. Then his

Defender of the Faith

only link with the past was the gold-hilted
sword propped in a corner. That congenial
air ripened his manhood. Days employed in protection softened him, and he
was unconsciously moulded by the moors
as they seemed happily supine in bright
weather or proud in resistance when the
winter was frantic.

Health made him restless; and he
would long to be powerful, as if some tall
ship sunk on its first adventure should
strain under insignificant keels. Then
peace made him quiet. The pride of his
youth had been broken, and he looked
up at life as the dead might study it from
under the scenes. Memory showed him
many dear once but not much to him now;
for they had loved a man who was gone.
Two were dear to him still, — a silent girl
with grey eyes, and a glad child; for his
love of them was stronger than Death.

Pilgrims of Grace

Often he would imagine his wife seated by the fire in their home while the glow fondled her silken hair as he used. Then he would feel Death and Sorrow were the shadowy things of a fireside dream.

Now he had done with anxiety, and his heart found repose in the comfortable belief of his fathers. To his chastened eyes the world had an unusual loveliness. In a hollow a waterfall seemed propping a wood. During still hours he watched it with an aching delight. At such times he was haunted by one of Mistress Anne's songs.

> "Somewhere in silent hills, a nook of trees
> Forgets this land of ills and little ease:
> My wanderings are blind, and full of care;
> And yet my heart shall find its country there."

The shepherd journeyed to market in the Spring and got news. So the Earl learnt how Aske had lifted the silver cross and

the banner of the Five Wounds on the
steps of York Cathedral, and had confronted the royal levies on the banks of
the Don, and how a miraculous rain had
flooded the river and had divided the
armies till the King had been able to
gather forces, and how the rebels had
separated, weakened by discord and en-
chanted by promises. Further he learnt
how Sir Francis Bigod had lifted the banner of the Five Wounds again, in spite of
the original leaders, and how Norfolk had
shattered the irresolute muster.

That autumn the shepherd fetched
sorrowful tidings. So the Earl learnt how
most of the original leaders had been
arrested in spite of the promised pardons,
and how the King had shouted, " Put an
end to them all ! Knit up the tragedy ! "
and how Lady Bulmer had been burnt
and Darcy beheaded and Aske hanged

Pilgrims of Grace

in York while Lady Northumberland was untouched in her home.

The old man recited these things merrily, contrasting the folly of great persons and the wisdom of sheep. Thus the Earl had a tardy knowledge of the affairs he had left. The death of Queen Jane in childbirth and the King's growing sickness and Cromwell's war with the nobles were little to him while his wife and daughter were free.

The shepherd sprained his ankle one Spring and was compelled to postpone his travels. Coming back from them gladly, he said he had gone out of his way to look at the spot where the Devil had swooped down on the Earl.

"Never did I enjoy myself so!" said he. "I thought of you also, for I was sure you would like to hear the Castle described. A mountainous building it is. There I saw a round little Friar."

"You spoke to him?" said Northumberland, eagerly.

"'A fine day,' says he, bobbing his head out of a window. 'It was raining early,' says I. 'That was but the pride of the morning,' says he."

"Did he say nothing else?"

"I am telling you all. 'What news?' says he. So I —"

"We can talk of that after. I want to hear what he said."

"How can I tell you if you keep interrupting? I did laugh! — Says he, 'You are lucky to see so much of the world.' 'It is my own doing,' says I, 'I am an adventurous voyager.' 'Ah!' says he, dolefully, 'but I am in prison.'"

"What?" said Northumberland, starting.

Pilgrims of Grace

"'In prison,' says he — his very words,
I assure you. 'What have you done?'
says I. 'Nothing,' says he. — He is
locked up for being mad, I thought. —
Says he, 'What are you laughing at?'
Says I to him, 'I was thinking of a
man I saw in the cage — lord! such vile
language!' 'I am caged, too,' says he.
'What are you grinning at now?' 'I
was thinking of a man that was fevered
and kept calling me Magdalen,' says I.
'Who was he?' says he, jumping. 'I
found him wounded over there, on the
night the Devil went off with the Traitor
Earl,' says I. 'And his name?' says
he frantically. 'Well, he answers to
Joseph,' says I, 'for I christened him so,
when he would not tell me —' 'What is
he like?' he screams. 'Tall and dark,'
says I, 'silent as a frog, and thin as a
crook, but companionable. This very

Defender of the Faith

hand he kissed — would you believe it? — calling me his beautiful wife Magdalen.' 'Oh, God be praised!' shrieked the Friar. I laughed till I was hardly able to stand."

"What did he say then?"

"'Where is he now?' says he. 'At my house,' says I. 'Where is that?' says he. Says I, 'Every one knows it — a matter of twenty miles away on the moors.' 'When are you going back?' says he. 'Please God, I'll sleep there to-night,' says I. 'Stop a minute,' says he, and rushes away."

"And then?" said Northumberland breathlessly.

"'For God's sake, I implore you to give him that,' says he, throwing something out of the window."

"What was it?"

"What do you think? Guess! The

Pilgrims of Grace

poor fellow seemed to think it was gold.
'I'll do it,' say I, picking it up, but
meaning to drop it as soon as I was out
of his sight. Mad as a hare he was, so —"

"But —"

"I tell you it was only a scrap of paper
folded up in a ball. I did laugh! He
fancied it was a diamond."

"Then you have lost it?"

"I meant to fling it away. Did I?
I pocketed it to please him, I know.
Ridiculous wretch! Wait," said the
shepherd, feeling his pocket, "I do believe I forgot to throw it away. No —
it is not there. — I suppose — Here the
thing is."

Northumberland snatched the paper
and opened it. A few words were
scrawled on it, "Lady Northumberland
is in the Tower, under sentence to be
burnt for High Treason."

Defender of the Faith

The shepherd went on, "'Tell your friend I'll wait at this window,' says the lunatic."

"Which window?" said Northumberland faintly.

"The one at the end of the Castle, near the bridge where the Devil — "

"I know it."

"I do believe he will wait."

Northumberland took his sword from the corner and belted it under his smock. Savagely bearded and clad as a shepherd, he was wholly disguised.

"Friend," said he softly, "I cannot thank you enough. If I live you'll see me again."

"You are not going?"

"At once."

"You are bewitched," cried the shepherd, crossing himself. "Why did I venture to that horrible place? The

Pilgrims of Grace

Friar was the Devil. I know it! How his eyes glittered!"

"Good-bye," said Northumberland, taking his crook and gripping his host's shrivelled hand.

"Joseph," the shepherd cried, "pray to be released from the spell. You will be torn limb from limb, Joseph!"

"Good-bye again," said Northumberland, going out of the hut.

"Your wealth?"

"Keep the few pieces if I never come back."

"I'll spend them in masses for your soul then; but it will be useless. You will be carried off; and the Devil will not take you to Purgatory. Kneel and try to pray, Joseph!"

As Northumberland went over the moor the old man cried peevishly, "Never say I left you unwarned. If you

Defender of the Faith

choose to go to the Devil it is nothing to
me." To prove how little he minded, he
began singing shrilly,

"A Scottish knight hoved on the bent,
A watch I dare well say ;
So was he ware on the noble Percy
In the dawning of the day."

Then Northumberland heard the feeble
voice break. When he looked back the
shepherd was crying.

In the early shine of the next morning
he saw the crowns of his towers. Because
there had been rain in the night they
shimmered and the woods had a fairy
tint and were sparkling. Then he heard
the fierce river.

As he crossed the wet bridge, he saw
the Friar peep out of the window and
look from him sadly, as if he hungered for
some one.

Pilgrims of Grace

" You have forgotten me ? " he said under the window.

With a cry of joy Friar Anderton peered, and then said sorrowfully, " You — like this ! — oh, my dear lord ! How you have suffered ! "

" Never more than now."

" But your coming will save her."

" What can I do against Cromwell ? "

" You can destroy him."

" I," said Northumberland, looking down at his smock.

" You, a bareheaded tattered shepherd, and I, an imprisoned Friar, shall conquer him. Deposuit potentes ! — Glory to God ! "

" Penniless — a voluntary outlaw — "

" I have gold," said the Friar, showing a bag. " My dear lady gave me all this to spend in charity, when she was arrested ; but I — "

Defender of the Faith

"That is of no use."

"It will furnish you with clothes and a horse."

"It will enable me to reach London more quickly. I can but share her fate."

"But you had no part in the Rising."

"My life threatens Cromwell. Yet if I could discover Augustine ——"

"He is dead."

"Then so is my last hope."

"No, for he died here."

"Under my roof?"

"Under Cromwell's," said the Friar. "Your property has been granted to him."

"He is welcome to it."

"It was given to him when your wife was condemned."

"When was that?"

"A fortnight ago."

Pilgrims of Grace

" When —"

" She was to suffer on the tenth."

" What day is this ? "

" Sunday the fourth."

" What month ? "

" June."

" The month we were married : it shall see us united."

" In this world. The light of God has dispelled the cloud of misunderstanding that severed you. From the bewildered twilight of youth you pass to the sober noon, she softened by grief and made wiser by solitude, and you no longer a jealous lover but a husband rejoicing in a quieter and trustful affection."

Northumberland looked down with a sigh.

" Your wife loves you with all her heart," said the Friar. " The stranger welcomed in sorrow was not misled by the

cold and weary face that belied her passionate tenderness. Wolsey sent me to
part you ; but I found you divided. I
believed you had told her of the betrothal
yourself. Daily I saw the trouble pass
beyond cure as custom made it familiar.
When Robert Aske spoke of it — My dear
lord, forgive me if I meddle with things
hallowed from strangers. You may — I
sometimes feared you thought she loved
Aske. As I hope to be saved, there was
but a friendship between them. Cold and
tender comrades — "

"That is all past."

"Not only her confessor, but her companion, I know how she clung to a hope.
When she heard your foster-brother had
vanished she was certain he had died
in your armour. Remembering how
strong he had been, she recalled your
exhaustion. Above all, she was sure

you would not have tried to kill Aske. 'That should have opened my eyes,' said she, 'though it embittered me then.'"

"Was Thorne's body found?"

"Shattered and beyond recognition."

"A loving friend."

"So was Aske's servant: he flung himself on his bed, saying, 'My master, my master! They will draw him, and hang him, and quarter him;' and thus he died of sorrow."

"God be with Robert Aske!"

"Your wife's heart was breaking when she doubted your love. When the truth was made evident she would have given her life to see you again. Long after I abandoned my hope of your coming she kept hers and found joy in that indestructible dream."

"And my child?"

"The Duke of Norfolk adopted her.

Defender of the Faith

This shall restore her to you," said the Friar as he held out a paper.

" What is it ? "

" Cromwell's death-warrant."

" What — "

" Erasmus said Englishmen live now as if a scorpion was under every stone, for they are in terror of Cromwell. Yet this — "

" What is it ? " repeated Northumberland.

" Come closer, my lord. Can you hear me ? It is Augustine's confession."

" Then I may deliver her — How did you — "

" Miserable Augustine repented. All this time Cromwell kept him hidden in Surrey. Cromwell is encompassed by foes : even the King loathes him, they say, and will buffet him and call him a

knave. Yet when he has been well pom-
melled and knocked about the head by
the King he will come out with as merry
a countenance as if he ruled all the roast.
Now he was afraid to keep Augustine
near London."

" Well ? "

"Augustine was taken ill here, and
believed he had been poisoned since
Cromwell dared not shelter him longer.
In the throes of death, he shrieked
for a priest till his gaolers were moved.
Poor wretches! Some beauty remains
in those defiled mirrors of God. So
they let me visit him, thinking it would
never be known. I could not absolve
him till he made some amends. He
wrote this, avowing he had poisoned
Queen Catherine by Cromwell's orders,
and had falsely accused Mistress Anne,
and had sold her a harmless love-philtre,

and had deceived her by writing incriminating words on the handkerchief."

" I was sure of it."

" Many suspected it: and here is the proof. Yet I feared it was worthless, for how could I have it sent to the King?"

" Where is he?"

" At Westminster."

" I lived in that house."

" Then you can reach him? 'How can I contend with the King?' the poor Cardinal used to say," said the Friar, as he thrust the paper into the bag. Throwing the bag down, he went on, " Now Cromwell will find the uselessness of contending with God."

Crossing the bridge, Northumberland took the road to the South. Keeping aloof from High-thorpe, he waded through Dead Man's Ford and arrived

Pilgrims of Grace

in Lincoln by night. There he was
shaved, and he purchased a black suit and
a horse. No one seemed to remember
him. As he took the London road in
the morning when the gate was opened he
felt he had no place in the world. Old
companions of his were intent on their
particular cares. Perhaps one or two of
them thought of him sometimes with a
moment's regret because he might have
been useful or pleasurable if he had lived.
Trapped in the nets of the world, why
should they squander thought on a man
incapable of hindrance or aid?

After his time on the moors the
meadows seemed haunts of a continual
summer. Fear was over those quiet
places; and the passers were silent,
shunning him with timorous looks.
When he drew rein on the hill-top by
Enfield and saw the ramparts and steeples

Defender of the Faith

of London and the prominent Tower he shivered. Instead of that rich city he saw robust Cromwell control England with implacable eyes.

Till then he had planned to seek the King instantly; but he altered his mind. Even if Cromwell fell would the King spare Lady Northumberland? Once he would have longed to avenge Mistress Anne; but he was quieted now. Infected by the popular fear, he determined to bid for Cromwell's assistance.

Riding into London, he saw yeomen in grey marbled liveries by Northumberland House. When he asked them whether the Lord Privy Seal was at home, they replied their master had gone to hear the Archbishop of Canterbury preach in the Abbey. So he passed out of the City by Ludgate, and went along Fleet Street to Charing Cross, and left his

horse at an inn, and walked to Westminster.

The royal standard was up, and troops
lined the thoroughfare in front of the
Palace. Between them, labourers were
planting a post. Heavy chains dangled
from the top of it, clattering. Could that
be the stake? he thought. Then he
reminded himself women were executed
at Smithfield. Besides, that day was only
the sixth of June — or had the Friar been
wrong?

"Cherry ripe! Cherry ripe!" called a
silver voice at his back.

A rosy golden-haired little girl in white
stood tendering a basket of fruit.

"Cherry ripe," she cried again, and
then shrank from him.

Said he, "What day of the month is it?"

"The sixth of June," she said pertly
as if she tried to be brave.

Defender of the Faith

"And when — when is Lady Northumberland to be — to be killed?"

"Next Saturday, sir," she said, beaming and regaining her courage. "Father is going to take me to see it."

"What are those men doing there?"

"You ought to ask them, not me. It looks as if they were going to burn somebody. Oh! I hope they are. I never saw — Oh, kind sir, will you lift me up if they do? But I must sell my basketful first, or father will beat me."

With that, she ran up the street, calling, "Ripe cherries! Cherry ripe!"

Then he looked at the Palace, and saw the King at a window. "Then he is in the Red Room? Small hope of mercy from him," said he to himself, as the King scowled at the work. So he went down to the Abbey.

CHAPTER III

Westminster Abbey was thronged, and
the preacher's voice sounded faint in the
shadows. Cromwell leant on a pillar as
if he listened with reverence. Wearing
his homespun and a short cloak with a
heavy collar of fur, he stood in a space.
Light streaming through the Rose window reddened him. Because his eyes
were cast down he seemed mild. Hearing the Earl's step, he uplifted them.
Still keeping his hands thrust in his
belt, he glanced at the others.

"Come," he said, and plodded apart.

As he turned into a nook the Earl
followed him. The preacher's far voice
came to them in a meaningless whisper.

249

Defender of the Faith

Said Cromwell, " I was thinking of you."

The Earl looked about him, recognising the chapel.

" Your father is there under your feet," Cromwell went on. " We are among the tombs of the Percies. I thought you had found a nameless grave in the North."

" I did," said Northumberland.

" But the grave gives up its dead? I am glad of it. Where were you lurking?"

" In the moors."

" I thought the tale of your death doubtful; so I let your wife live. When her danger did not bring you —"

" I heard of it a couple of days ago."

" Too soon. If you had delayed you would have come to life free. A man fighting the world should not be hampered by guarding a perishable flower."

" I want to live in peace."

Pilgrims of Grace

"A wish marvellous on the lips of a Percy. Here your kinsmen are quiet. Your father is peaceful, being dead."

"I come to insist upon your freeing my wife."

"There is fight in you still."

"I can force you — "

"Many have tried."

"I have a weapon."

"That sword? — Wolsey's gift. What became of the Cardinal?"

"I have another."

"Eh? One more alarming? The great Marquis of Exeter stabbed me at a Council: his dagger broke on my hidden breastplate, and I put him to sleep. Did you see Augustine?"

"No."

"Then your weapon is blunt. I was never afraid. Yet the remembrance of two annoyed me with a trifling uneasi-

Defender of the Faith

ness. I liked them both, as it happened.
You and my old friend Augustine — ”

“ I am proud of your liking, and the
more when you couple me with that
infamous poisoner.”

“ His trade was to use medicines for
the fever of life. Yet his nature was
tender: I have seen him cherish his
family with animal love. I wish I could
have let him return to Venice; but his
knowledge was dangerous. It was all I
could do to keep him safe from the
King. I shall not profit by his witchcraft again. Do you remember that
pleasant device of mine, the Magical
Mirror? I had put a sheet of glass in
front of the hidden door; and there was
the Concubine, dim on the steps, while
behind her I watched you and his
Majesty gaping dumfounded — Well,
you and Augustine might have vexed

me together; but you earned his dis-
like, — you sent him to London fastened
under a horse. Now he is gone. You
did not meet him?"

" Friar Anderton did."

"Eh? Anderton? Oh, yes! a garrulous simpleton — I locked him up because he was a friend of your wife's.
How could they meet? They were con-
fined to their rooms."

" Augustine begged for a priest."

" When he was dying? The guards
gave way? At every step I am thwarted
by the ineradicable superstitions of
fools! Have you seen Friar Anderton?
How?"

" I was under his window."

" Where were the sentries? "

" In front of the Castle. The window
was high."

" I thought you liked him."

Defender of the Faith

"I do."

"Yet now you sentence him to be hanged from that window."

"Unless you go to the Block."

"Eh? Augustine signed a confession? You have it?"

"Perhaps."

"I wish to know."

"So I thought," said Northumberland.

"Well, I admit your weapon is keen. What do you want?"

"My wife's freedom."

"She was a rebel."

"You overlooked it till you needed my wealth."

"I overlook nothing," said Cromwell. "When the lapse of time made your disappearance seem permanent —"

"You seized my estate."

"There was no son to inherit. Wealth has advantages."

Pilgrims of Grace

"You can keep most of mine. . Give me back Wharfe."

"You endeavour to bribe me? For your sake I tampered with justice and postponed her deserts. Now she must die. It is necessary."

Northumberland was going away; but Cromwell said quickly, "A minute! We may yet come to terms. You saved me on the night of the first Rising of the Pilgrims of Grace."

"I regret it."

"I had gone to the North secretly, to discover how matters stood, since I never trust a subordinate. Finding the rebellion inevitable, I maimed it by choosing Aske as a leader. Those addresses purporting to be signed by him were written by me."

"Aske disowned them."

"Yet when he was hailed as the leader

he accepted the post. So I furnished
the rebels with a captain inexperienced
in war and law-abiding and scrupulous
and reluctantly obeyed by the nobles.
I was on my way to your house; but
the premature beacons — "

"What has this to do — ?"

"The Cardinal and the Concubine and
Darcy and Aske rest as little children
sleep. Here am I still toiling apart.
The muddy gardener digs while the
lovers gather the roses."

"Not a gardener, but a grave-digger."

"Seeds are planted in graves. Weed-
ing England, I have not spared crowned
thistles. If I lived for myself I would
share the happy discontent of my bees,
and cultivate whimsical pansies and that
singular vegetable, the rhubarb, discovered in Barbary by Andreas Boorde.
I think if I planted it — I have been too

given to solitude. Falls teach a child to stand ; but our blunders enrich us with desirable wisdom when it is vain. I once sought a helper, the Concubine."

"You murdered that unfortunate lady."

" The wine of love changes into vinegar often. Mated with her, I would have set the world· free. We are all linked together. Women mould us in darkness, from the womb to the tomb."

" If you cannot speak to the purpose —"

"When a man is feeble his mould is effeminate and his stains are enduring. You and I remember the King a castle of flesh, a lord of strenuous brutes. Misery and sickness have levelled him with the vilest of women. Now he is conscious of defilement and brimming with a hate of himself that overflows against all, and a womanish cruelty is his

Defender of the Faith

predominant passion. The Rose Decorate of England is festering. What is
the gardener's task?"

"The King is my master."

"And mine, I am afraid. Brainsick
women subdue me. If I could prolong
his suffering for a couple of years, I could
resist his authority. Daily I grow richer,
and stronger in the love of the people.
As the months pass I thin the ranks of
the nobles. Never so much in love with
the world, freed from the trammels of
selfish longings and only striving to make
humanity fortunate, — must I yield now?
Sunset sees rosy windows. When one
hope perishes another deludes us, like a
toy dangled out of reach of a baby. If
we did not hope to be free, we would be
reconciled to chains and abandon frus-
trate toil. If I could have two little
years! The King turns on me, because

Pilgrims of Grace

I found him a hideous wife, Anne of Cleves."

" Is he married ? "

" Not at the moment. The day after her arrival he wanted to behead her for treason."

" What was her crime ? "

" Presuming to marry him without changing her looks. Because she was a German he had to wed her by proxy. How could I guess her portrait was flattering ? "

" But I cannot believe — " said the Earl.

" The alleged treason was the possible fact that she had been betrothed to another. The old story again ! Well, she saved her neck by consenting to an immediate divorce. Now he has soft eyes for that imp, Catherine Howard."

" Poor girl ! I remember her."

" The child plots with Norfolk and

Defender of the Faith

Rich. Because I can prove she was betrothed she has resolved to destroy me.
My surest revenge is to let her marry the
King. When he tires of her she goes
to the block. If I sought now to
cross his whim I would fail, but after
the wedding. — If she can compass my
death I shall bequeath the proof to a
friend. I have toiled night and day and
denied myself everything. The fruit of my
labour is a tragical comedy of varying love."

"Why should she wish —"

"A guttering candle is still deadly to
moths. What would she not give to
possess the jewelled crown for a week
among her envious rivals? No doubt,
she is confident her sway will be lasting.
The King is great in disaster, — miserably
removed above all. Children huddle
under the oaks : who shall give shelter to
the kings of the forest? Tainted by

hereditary rottenness, he writhes eaten by
ulcers, the fruit of his congenital vices.
Crazed by thwarted passion, and miserly,
and raging alone — the most unhappy of
kings!"

"God pity him! But he was never a
miser."

"Lavishness brought him the humilia-
tion of poverty. Now his bitter pleasures
are cruelty and gathering riches. Wolsey
pampered him with the goods of the
Church. I won power by betraying the
secret of the Cardinal's wealth. In turn
I provided the King with all the gold of
the monasteries."

"And you must answer for it."

"I am ready to answer for every act of
my life. 'The Hammer of the Monks'
they have called me. If a monk was a
saint I delivered him from the tempta-
tions of riches; if he was a sinner I disen-

Defender of the Faith

tangled him from the need of hypocrisy;
if he was, like most of us, neither evil nor
good I loosed him from unnatural vows.
How the rejoicing Gods mock unprofit-
able attempts to be virtuous!"

"The Gods? You are a heathen now?
I have heard you croak hymns to Our
Lady."

"Seeking myself under my many
masks, I found God. The Word is the
Life. Now I see God in everything, life
in stones, birth in corruption. Worship-
pers kneel to themselves. Yet the vulgar
need threats of damnation. For their
sake I assume convenient religions."

"You have persecuted — "

"Tilling is killing. A spade must
bring disaster to worms. The clod and
the worm are as divine as the gardener.
What is more splendid than a thistle in
bloom? Yet — "

Pilgrims of Grace

" I think you talk to detain me."

" Eh? The King craves for gold, and so I begged your estate."

" Then why did he grant it to you? "

" As he preferred to induce Wolsey to surrender his hoards, so he covets mine as a compulsory gift. There is always a risk that he may incline to take my head with my purse. Well! Yonder is the fatal and huge wreck of a King. Here am I loved by the people because I make ninepins of redoubtable nobles, and especially honoured by the Lutherans since I am their shield and saintly Latimer's friend. There my enemies listen to the Archbishop of Canterbury. ' Can the blind lead the blind? do they not both then fall into the ditch? ' — that was his text, and it made me deaf to his sermon. Should any man strive to lead the rest in the dark and govern the in-

tangible images of a Magical Mirror?
I begin to be aware of my blindness.
Still I had rather lead than obey. Prince
Edward is a puling and sickly child, and
the King's daughters are declared illegiti-
mate. After the King some man will
govern as Protector : if I did, it would
provoke civil war; but the gentlemen
will submit to a noble. Some great lord
will be master. Who? Perhaps the
Earl of Northumberland?"

"I have no such ambition."

"I want an ally —"

"Then —"

"This purpose has been long in my
head. The Concubine sundered us, and
then came the Rising. It is good fishing
in troubled waters ; and I chose that
occasion for offering you half of my
power. I could not see you in prison
without Kingston's knowledge, and so

Pilgrims of Grace

I meant to find you at Wharfe. This is an appropriate place for that desired understanding. Here soldiers and priests and rebels and sovereigns rest from their foolery. 'This is the final concord,' as lawyers write at the beginnings of deeds. I offer to deliver your wife and make you Protector. I proffer the Crown. The King is dying. The Prince cannot live long; if he does there may be found ways— Your fathers rivalled the imperious Plantagenets. Would they have shrunk from replacing a degenerate Tudor?"

"Your offer is an insult —"

"You had a drawback, for you looked down on the people. Hiding among them, you must have learnt the value of men unthwarted by schooling, sturdy folk roughly made of the soil of wholesome England. I am one of them, and it is my pride —"

Defender of the Faith

"You an Englishman? Soaked in Italian venom!—"

"Foreign influence liberates England. What is the King but a fantastical Welshman?—I have found Machiavelli too subtle for these moderate brains. Placid England abhors difficult wisdom. I 'll take no hurried denial. Think it over at leisure."

"Once and for all, I refuse," said Northumberland. "I have humbled myself for the sake of my wife; but she would not wish me to rescue her at the price of dishonour. I can but appeal to the King. If he is merciless—as I fear—I can die with her."

"I am not angry, my lord. My blood is common and sluggish. I am sorry you are dooming yourself. I cannot afford to let you live as my enemy. You may think better of it. Linger till the sermon is over."

As Northumberland turned out of the

chapel, Cromwell went on, " I might as
well appeal to your fathers : they will not
throb, though you toss the banner of the
White Lion or shout ' Esperance Percy.' "

Northumberland passed through the
congregation again, and as he went out
looked back and saw Cromwell had not
returned to the pillar. Hastening, he
found a mob had assembled by the post
in the street, and saw Rich and Mistress
Catherine Howard on the steps of the
Palace. Rich seemed older and anxious ;
but the girl was as pretty and plump as
ever, and her daring blue eyes twinkled
with mischief as she stood in white, toy-
ing with a bunch of red roses.

The yeomen on guard refused to let
the Earl pass, and so he called out to
Rich. After staring incredulously Rich
ran down and made the sentries stand back.

Defender of the Faith

"I have to see the King at once," said the Earl.

"I fear it is impossible," Rich answered sweetly. "My honoured friend, the Lord Privy Seal, has put guards before the Red Room, and allows no one—"

"I think I can enter it in spite of the guards."

"I wish I could."

"Come with me," said the Earl.

Bowing to Mistress Catherine, he went up the back stairs.

"Can there be a hidden door?" said Rich eagerly.

"Here it is, and unlocked."

"My kind lord, I hope your business will prosper," said Rich. "I must go back to our fair friend, Mistress Howard."

Northumberland went down the dark steps, and lifted the tapestry.

CHAPTER IV

CLAD in yellow, the King hobbled at the other side of the room, dragging his ulcerated leg. Northumberland shrank as if he looked on a leper. Then pity mingled with that involuntary shudder of hate. Tears came to his eyes as he remembered his comrade.

The King paused by the window, and then drew himself up as there was cheering outside. Nodding affably, he hummed gruffly,

" Le temps s'en va,
   Le temps s'en va, ma dame.
La ! Le temps non, mais nous nous en allons."

Turning his back to the window, he bowed his head, shutting his eyes, and thrusting out his clenched hands. Then he looked up. Reeling back, he opened his hands wide, and then crossed himself while his lips quivered as if he muttered a prayer. The people began cheering again as he looked at Northumberland sidelong.

"Did Anne send you to warn me?" he whispered.

"I came to implore mercy," said Northumberland, kneeling.

"They told me you were dead," cried the King, facing him.

"I was in hiding."

"God's wounds! you would have been wiser to stay so!" cried the King, in a rasping voice. "Do you think me dying, since you —"

"I could not reach you otherwise. Cromwell has forbidden the yeomen to let anyone pass."

Pilgrims of Grace

"Give orders here?   Rise."

Said Northumberland sadly, as he rose, "I have heard you are ailing."

"It is nothing.   I 'll be well soon. My heart is sick, Harry.   Why did you hide?   All shrink from me now."

"I hid from myself. "

"Poor boy!" said the King, crossing the room with his old swagger, yet wincing as if he mastered his pain.

"You are altered," he went on, laying his hands heavily on Northumberland's shoulders.   "Yes, you had troubles.   I have a royal portion: I would mind nothing if I could only be well."   Sighing, he took the gilt chair.   "My sickness is trifling.   The doctors say they can cure me.   Ignorant liars! Another voice whispers, 'You are dying!'   It will never be still.   It wakes me at night. It is soft; but it echoes above shout-

271

ing and trumpets. When you saw me last I was the proudest King in the world. Now I am sick and shunned and a laughing-stock! Well, what do you ask? It shall be granted, for the sake of old brotherhood."

"Your Grace, I beg for a life," said Northumberland, kneeling.

"Some criminal's," said the King, lazily. "He shall be pardoned. I have sent sinners enough before me to Judgment."

"A woman's life."

"Ha! I remember," said the King, shutting his eyes. Peering up under his heavy and red eyelids, he went on very slowly, "I wait to see your wife burn."

"Oh God! the doom was not for to-day!"

"I hurried it. I was afraid I might die. As I am unable to go to Smithfield,

the Stake has been put where I can watch
it. There are not many pleasures sweet
to the King."

" Have mercy ! " Northumberland cried,
clasping his hands.

" I loved a woman once, and sent
her to death. I shall not spare another.
You see me tortured, wrecked in body
and soul. Even in this world women
have damned me. I speak from my
heart, Harry, for we used to be
friends."

" For the sake of that kindness ! "

" Poor lad ! " said the King, putting
his arm round Northumberland's neck.
" You might have moved me once. The
icy clutch of Death freezes my heart. "
Drawing his arm back, he went on,
" Rise ! she shall suffer."

" For God's sake ! "

" Cromwell proved — Where is that

knave? Awaiting him, I left that door open. Even he begins to avoid me. Stand up, I say."

" Then I rise to impeach him."

" A forlorn hope."

" I can make his infamy evident."

" What need of that? The dog is true to his master."

" Most false to you."

" Ha! Make your words good."

" I accuse him of murder."

" He and I have killed many."

" You have crushed rebels ; but he poisoned a Queen."

" What Queen?" the King said with a shudder.

" Queen Catherine."

" The Lady Catherine of Arragon was my bitterest foe."

" And he sent another Queen to the Block."

Pilgrims of Grace

" That was my doing."

" But his charges were false."

" I loved you and Norris and Anne.
You are here. · Never speak of those
others if you value your life."

" I value it no longer."

" Anne! — poor sinful child! I wish
I could hear her laughing again, —
even at my tragedies. Many things
were dear to her — warmth and light,
luxury and flattering whispers. The
grave is black and cold. You loved
her, and then I hated you for it.
Still we may be united by a common
regret."

" I can prove she was guiltless of
poisoning — "

" Then no torture would suffice for
your punishment."

" Work your will on me, but first I
shall speak. There was a time when

your meanest subject could appeal to your justice. I, no mean subject—"

"That time is over."

"Here is dead Augustine's confession."

"Give it to me," said the King, holding out his hand feebly. Taking the confession, he tore it, and threw the scraps away as if they were poisoned. "Thus she tore Catherine's letter," he went on while his small mouth and his bulging cheeks quivered and his eyes became dim.

There was a step in the passage behind him, and he turned painfully with a smile on his lips. "Here he comes," he said softly.

Then Rich lifted the arras. The King started, and Rich fell on his knees.

"Your Grace, pardon me for coming unbidden," said Rich, trembling. "It is a matter of life and death."

Pilgrims of Grace

"You may find it so. What is your errand?"

"I come to accuse my Lord Privy Seal —"

"It never rains but it pours," the King growled, leaning back. "What misled you to come here unannounced?"

"He has forbidden —"

"Ha! So I heard. All this time, he said the courtiers were shunning me."

"Because he kept them aloof," said Northumberland.

"Good!" said the King sleepily. "What are the charges?"

Said Rich, "My Lord Cromwell has taken bribes from your enemies —"

"So do all that can."

"And using such malicious words as were abominable to hear, said he would fight sword in hand —"

"Spade in hand, you mean."

277

Defender of the Faith

"— if your Grace varied in religious opinions, and said he trusted to bring matters to such a frame that your Majesty could no longer resist him if he should live for a year or two."

"But he may not live a year."

"Further, he has befriended the heretics."

"Ha!"

"And has disseminated erroneous books denying the doctrine of the Real Presence."

"Prove that," cried the King, "and he shall go to the Tower."

"Here are the depositions."

"Numerous. Rise. Put them there. I shall read them. You know their truth?"

"Surely," said Rich.

"Is the fox caught at last? Who are the witnesses to the words you have quoted?"

"The Duke of Norfolk."

Pilgrims of Grace

" An enemy."

" And I am another."

" A friend."

" While he was loyal," said Rich.

" Ha! Cromwell said you have been much with Mistress Catherine lately. The child avenges her cousin. Cromwell brought More to the block with the help of those ears. You can still hear all you want? You are enviable." With that he glanced at Northumberland. " Who is the worst enemy? — a treacherous friend," he muttered, stooping over the papers. First, he stared at them heavily, as if he was blind; then beginning to read, he flushed, scowling, and kept turning them over. " A heretic!" he grumbled — " a pestilent and damnable heretic! Summon the Council!" he cried furiously as he hammered the table.

As Rich hurried out, the King looked

Defender of the Faith

at Northumberland. "You have not called for justice in vain," he said. "This base-born adventurer has ruled me too long. Pick up those scraps, and cast them out of the window."

As the Earl gathered the fragments of Augustine's confession and crossed the room the King leant on the table and propped his eyes on his hands. "Vicegerent of the Head of the Church," he muttered, "and a heretic. ' God's Vicegerent,' they called him the other day at the Council. Did they put him in my place? Or did they hail me as God? If they were right, I would doom myself; but I think I would let Anne have her way. What are they doing out there?" he went on, looking up.

"Piling the fagots round the Stake," said the Earl, flinging the scraps out of the window. "Let me go now."

Pilgrims of Grace

"To your wife? It is not time yet. I shall deal with her afterwards."

There was great cheering outside.

"They love you," said the King, with a scowl.

Said the Earl, "Cromwell approaches, trudging with unusual haste."

"How does he look?"

"Ruddy and prosperous. The people surround him: he is shaking their hands."

"The Cardinal rode through them, smelling his aromatical orange to overcome their poisonous breath. Cromwell felled Wolsey. In his turn, he is betrayed by a friend. So the Fates weave their web: they have entangled me also. Like Œdipus, I found myself ignorantly guilty of incest. Like Philoctetes, I am forsaken to agony."

"Now he smiles no more," said Northumberland.

Defender of the Faith

" Has somebody warned him ? "

" He saw me."

" A death's head at the window. Why has the cheering stopped ? "

" Because he is aghast."

" Rats leave a sinking ship."

" Now he turns, — he retreats."

" Stop him ! " cried the King. " Call out to them to arrest him. They will not hear you. Summon —"

" No need. Rich hastens out, calls to him. Cromwell turns back uneasily."

" Well ? "

" Rich runs to him, — bows, full of sweetness and reverence."

" A pleasant knave," said the King, chuckling. " I shall make him Lord Chancellor. — Ha ! They are shouting."

" Louder than ever, and tossing their caps in the air. Cromwell comes smiling."

Pilgrims of Grace

" He shall never be cheered again," said the King.

"Stand here," he went on. "Arrest him, when I lift my right hand. Say nothing till I give you the signal."

Then an usher announced Norfolk. The King sat erect, squaring his shoulders and spreading his right hand on the table while his left clutched his dagger. Norfolk and five other lords came in, clad sumptuously, bending their knees. Seeing Northumberland on the King's right, they exchanged wondering glances. Then they paused by the table, with their eyes on the King; but he kept his on the documents.

"Room for my Lord Privy Seal," cried the usher.

Cromwell tramped in, followed by Rich. The King looked up gladly, with his kindliest smile.

Defender of the Faith

"Ha! my trusty servant," he said, "my loving Vicegerent."

As he held out his left hand Cromwell knelt, kissing it. Norfolk glanced at Rich with alarm. Rich turned white and looked back as if he thought of escaping.

"My only friend," said the King, hugging Cromwell's thick neck, "take your accustomed seat."

Brushing against Northumberland as if he did not observe him, Cromwell sat down clumsily, and stared at the others with a humorous malice.

"What could I do without your assistance?" the King muttered, scowling at his bloated right hand. "Henry of England is feeble and surrounded by traitors. Be seated, my lords."

So they took their seats, watching him. Cromwell flung back his cloak, disclosing the jewel of the George, and shot a glance at the papers, and then thrust his hands in his belt comfortably, and studied the King. On his right Norfolk sat rigid.

"I am merciful, my lords," said the King, clenching his fist.

"All the world knows it, your Grace," said Norfolk, tugging his beard.

"I must be, since this hand has grown weak. I am long-suffering and forgetful of injuries. Calumny has not turned me aside. Mordear opprobriis falsis, — shall I change colour though I am bitten by unmerited blame? I am above the scope of liars. Yet if my friend is calumniated I may be harsh. My Lord Privy Seal has been insulted by slanderers. I should be loth to believe one of my Council had taken part with his enemies. Does any one dare accuse him now to his face?"

Rich opened his mouth as if he was going to speak, and then looked at Norfolk.

Defender of the Faith

The Earl stood with arms folded as he watched the King's hand. Cromwell glanced up at him, and then paled; for he saw Mistress Catherine Howard lifting the tapestry.

"No one?" said the King, looking up.

"I dare," cried Mistress Catherine, stepping into the room. As the King started and scowled at her she stood on his left fearlessly and pointed at Cromwell.

"I denounce him as a heretic and a rebel," she said.

"What brings you here?" cried the King, lifting his hand as if he was going to strike her.

"My Lord Privy Seal, I arrest you of Treason," said Northumberland, gripping Cromwell's left arm.

As Cromwell and the rest of the Council

sprang to their feet the King muttered,
" I gave the signal. — Out of the mouths
of children."

"What does this mean, your Grace?"
stammered Cromwell.

The King peered at him, smiling.

" Is this the reward of all my service?"
gasped Cromwell.

The King nodded.

" On your conscience, I ask you am I
a traitor?" cried Cromwell. " I may
have offended, but never with my will.
Those that meddle with many matters
cannot answer for them all. Such faults
as I may have committed are deserving of
pardon."

" Such pardon as you have granted to
others," cried Norfolk fiercely, snatching
the George from Cromwell's neck. " Your
Grace, let him be judged by his own laws.
He has twisted idle words into Treason.

Defender of the Faith

Let the measure he has dealt to the innocent be meted to him!"

Said the King, smiling at Cromwell, "Forgiveness is injustice. You shall be judged by your own law of Attainder."

"I claim a trial," said Cromwell.

"I have not used that law; but now I give you its benefit. You shall be doomed without a chance to defend yourself. Then it shall be repealed, for this hand is strong enough to govern without it."

"Then," said Cromwell as if he was choking, "make quick work, without leaving me to languish in prison."

"I grant your last request," said the King. Waving his hand, he went on: "To the Tower with him! My Lords, you are dismissed."

Cromwell lurched out of the room, staggering as if he was drunk. The rest of the Council knelt, and hurried after him gladly.

"What is to be done with this puppet?" the King growled as he rose.

"What the King chooses," said Mistress Catherine, smiling up at him roguishly.

"A saucy miscreant," he muttered, laying his left hand on her shoulder.

"A worshipping slave," she said softly.

"Does she worship the sick man or the King?"

"Both," she said with tears in her eyes.

"No tears!" he said. "What shall I call you? Not Catherine. Catherine of Arragon was an honourable and virtuous wife."

"You doubt me?" she sobbed.

Defender of the Faith

"I am too old to bandy compliments, child. So this was your work? You hate Cromwell?"

"With good cause," she said, flushing.

"A bold infant."

"Howards are not cowards," said she.

"Very true," he said grimly. "Anne was courageous. But they may dare too much."

"I fear nothing," said she.

"You brave me?" he said furiously, clutching her.

"Because I love you," she whispered.

"I wish I believed it."

"You hurt me," she said wincing.

"A delicate baby," he said, drawing her to him.

"If I was a craven, would I tremble when I can hide in your heart?"

"You will be safe if you can enter that refuge. God help you, if you fail!"

Pilgrims of Grace

" Am I far from it now? " she whispered, leaning her little head on his breast.

" Once upon a time," he said slowly, " a lion lay wounded to death, and all the world kept from his reach till a mouse frolicked under his paw. I think he loved that tiny mouse for a minute. Then his maimed paw sank."

" Give me the minute's love," she sobbed. " Crush me, then, oh, my King ! "

" Come closer to my heart. Use drugs to make me love you; employ witch-craft," he muttered, putting his other arm about her and hugging her. " I am weary of hating."

Drums rolled in the distance. Northumberland had been looking on sadly. Starting, he went to the window. The King thrust the girl away, and she tottered.

Defender of the Faith

"The soldiers," said the Earl, as the drums were louder and a trumpet was blown.

"Women! foul apes!" the King muttered. "Quick!" he whispered, almost shutting his eyes. "Run to the door, child, lock it, bring me the key —"

As she obeyed him and he put the key in his breast, the hammering grew.

"They bring her to die!" groaned Northumberland.

Running back, he knelt to the King.

"Take my life, but spare hers," he cried.

"Why should I hurt you?" said the King, tenderly. "You liked me once. You loved Anne. That was natural. It was unfortunate that your acquaintance with her should have begun her destruction. Now you have convinced me that I destroyed her unjustly. I did not read the confession, yet I believed it. That knowledge will make my remaining time trebly delicious. You have many claims to my gratitude."

Northumberland bowed his head.

"Here is my ring. I stole it from Anne in days when we were happy together. Run, dearest friend. Take this to Kingston as a token that you come in my name."

"Your Grace!" said Northumberland, looking up wildly.

"Tell him I spare your wife. Go back to the North and the joys of innocent love."

"God reward you for this," sobbed the Earl, kissing the King's hand with uncontrollable tears.

Seizing the ring, he ran across to the door. The King watched him and smiled.

"The door is locked!" cried Northumberland as he shook it in vain.

Defender of the Faith

The King put his hands on his hips, and threw his head back and laughed.

"Guards! Open the door!" shouted Northumberland.

"Oh, this is horrible!" sobbed Mistress Catherine, shuddering away from the King.

"I have not laughed so for ages," he gasped. "I have the key, Harry."

"This is your revenge," the Earl whispered.

"Shout from the window! If they hear you they will think you are mad. Try this favourite hidden door if you can pass me."

Northumberland strode back to the King. "You were my friend," he said, gripping his hilt.

"And I hate you all the more," the King muttered.

"But you are my King," cried the Earl, tossing his hands up in despair.

Pilgrims of Grace

"And I crush you," the King shouted,
stamping. Then he writhed hideously,
and lifted his foot. "Forget all that,"
he cried. "We are men, face to face.
You are strong, loving; I — as you
see. You have a sword. Strike! I 'll
thank you for it."

"I 'll not raise my hand against you."

"Loathsome coward !"

"But I will," cried Mistress Catherine.
Springing between them, she snatched
Northumberland's sword. "I 'll strike
unless you give me the key," she sobbed,
lifting it up.

"Rebellious mite !" said the King.

"A mere woman — an ape ! " she
sobbed.

"A pretty one."

With her left hand she snatched the
key from his breast. "Take it," she
said, giving it to Northumberland. "Set

Defender of the Faith

your wife free. Stop him if you dare," she went on, pointing the shaking sword at the King.

Laughing loud, he glanced at Northumberland. " Off with you, Harry!" he said. " Save your wife. Never let me see you again."

As she dropped the sword, he held out his arms to her.

" Come closer to my heart," said the King.

SOME PRESS OPINIONS.

A CHILD IN THE TEMPLE.

Mr. Frank Mathew has shown himself the possessor of a rare and subtle individuality. He has caught the Celtic spirit; and in his work there is always the evasive, enchanting savor, the suggestion of childlike simplicity mingled with a wisdom that has brooded for ages, which leads one to think at once of that inexplicable gift called genius. — CHARLES G. D. ROBERTS, *in the Illustrated American.*

THE WOOD OF THE BRAMBLES.

The book displays the vivid descriptive power and rugged strength of a high-pitched and intensely dramatic imagination. — *The Times.*

One of the quaintest and most delightful of books. — *Athenæum.*

A work which should place the author in the position of *the* Irish novelist of the day. — *Whitehall Review.*

A book which is predestined to fame. It is unfair to class Mr. Mathew as the Kipling or the Barrie of Ireland; his individuality is all his own. — *Vanity Fair.*

This book carries the rare stamp of a temperament. Mr. Mathew brings you a whole world, — the quaint, pathetic, and yet noble and gallant world of Ireland in the last century. — RICHARD LE GALLIENNE, *in Idler.*

AT THE RISING OF THE MOON.

For literary capital, Mr. Frank Mathew has a good deal of mother-wit, with much quiet humour, and a particularly intimate knowledge of his country. Nothing Irish seems alien to him. All the stories are marked by grace and moderation of style. — *Bookman.*

Ireland has found her Kipling. The very heart of Ireland beats in the stories, and every figure abounds with character. — *Boston Herald.*